G000280539
OF THE ROYAL NAVY
SINCE 1945
By Lt. Cdr. David Hobbs RN
Introduction by Rear Admiral
A.R. Rawbone C.B., A.F.C.

FOREWORD

BY REAR ADMIRAL
A.R. RAWBONE
CB, AFC

This fascinating book reflects the care taken by the author in compiling authentic details.

At first sight it may appear to be a book for the specialist—but through its pages all interested in Naval matters can trace the trauma of Fleet Air Arm history which recently culminated in the brilliant success of the Falklands Campaign.

Ever since 1945 in the battle for an adequate slice of the Defence Budget our three Services have understandably disagreed on fundamentals. Within the Navy itself there has been disagreement over priorities. This has inevitably had its affect on Naval aircraft and specified roles.

HM Ships EAGLE and ARK ROYAL, our two main Fleet Carriers during the period covered were laid down during the last world war and commissioned in the early 1950's. They were soon outdated and modernisation programmes hardly kept pace with the increased size, weight and sophistication of successive aircraft. Thus aircrew, aircraft handlers and the whole host of supporting personnel became adept at improving and operating within very fine limits.

Many aircraft were totally inadequate for the tasks assigned, other surprised by their ease of handling and adaptability. Today the Harrier is unique and has fortunately proved itself in all weathers, operating from small carriers which themselves were not designed to provide full air cover over the Fleet.

Each aircraft has a story of its own. Many conclusions can be drawn but the thread of history runs throughout the text and is a tribute to Lieutenant Commander Hobb's dedication to an elite arm of the service of which he is a member.

Ray Rawbone

The Fleet Air Arm is an integral and essential part of the Royal Navy. Its aircraft are capable of operating from the decks of a large variety of ships, even in the most extreme weather conditions. No fleet can hope to operate without controlling the surface, the depths beneath it and the air above—as the Falklands Campaign has so clearly shown.

The period since the end of the Second World War has not been one of continuous peace. Aircraft of the Royal Navy have seen action in a variety of theatres including Malaya, Korea, Suez, Kuwait, East Africa, Borneo, Aden, Northern Ireland and the South Atlantic. The different roles played by naval aircaft in these actions show the necessity for a balanced force of fixed wing aircraft and helicopters capable of fulfilling a wide range of tasks.

Since 1945 there have been a number of fundamental changes. A post war rundown was followed by a period of stability during which the Royal Navy was re-equipped with some of the finest military aircraft and helicopters in the world. These served in a stable force of well equipped carriers. The 1957 Defence White Paper drastically reduced all the Services. The Fleet Air Arm suffered from the loss of carriers and aircraft held in reserve together with the disbanding of all RNR Air Squadrons. The decision about a replacement class of carriers was also delayed. The Front Line Squadrons remained relatively unscathed and by 1966 had reached a peak of tactical skill and professionalism unmatched by any other Navy in the world. This made the political decision, in the 1966 Defence Review, not to order the replacement carriers of the CVA01 Class seem a shattering blow. The rundown of the carriers and their air groups resulting from this Defence Review was in some part offset by the creation of an anti-submarine helicopter force capable of operating from ships other than aircraft carriers. The Fleet was, however, left unbalanced and vulnerable to air attack.

Depressing as this period was, commonsense eventually prevailed and a new generation of ships was created with HMS INVINCIBLE, the first of a new class of light fleet carriers, being laid down in 1973. The order for the first batch of the remarkable Sea Harrier fighter followed in 1975. Constant improvement to the Sea King force and the introduction to the service of the Lynx helicopter in small ships have also helped to restore to the Royal Navy a Fleet Air Arm capable of playing its proper role in a balanced fleet at sea.

The Fleet Air Arm today is small but just as professional as ever. With guided weapons and torpedoes it packs a terrific punch. The loss of HMS ARK ROYAL and her aircraft in 1978 is still keenly felt however since, when she paid off, we lost not just a weapon but a whole arsenal. No attempt was made to replace the Gannet AEW3 and its all seeing radar capable of locating ships up to 200 miles away and aircraft at more than 100 miles. This clearly was a mistake that must be remedied, and useful as the hastily converted AEW Sea King is proving to be it cannot fully match the potential of a new fixed wing AEW aircraft. This would also, of course, have great potential in roles, such as electronic warfare and air to air tanker, absent from the Fleet at present. The Sea Harrier has proved itself to be an outstanding multi role combat aircraft but it falls far short of the specialist capabilities of the Buccaneer and Phantom that it replaced.

For the future, nothing is ever certain. The South Atlantic Campaign proved, once again, that a fleet cannot hope to operate on the high seas without its own embarked aircraft. Let us hope that the lesson has now finally been taken to heart and that constant improvements, new aircraft and ships will be continually forthcoming.

In the following pages you will find a wide range of aircraft that have served in the Royal Navy since 1945—to the present day.

The opinions expressed in the notes are the personal views of the Author.

BLACKBURN FIREBRAND

Variants TF4 TF5
Role Torpedo Strike Fighter
Engine 1 x 2520 hp Bristol Centaurus IX
Span 51′3½″ **Length** 38′9″ **Max Weight** 16,700 lbs.
Max Speed 380 knots **Crew** Pilot
Armament 4 x 20 mm cannon in wings. 1 x Mk 15 or 17 torpedo, 1 x 2000 lb. or 1000 lb. bomb, 1 x Mk 6, 7 or 9 mine, 1 x 100 gallon drop tank on the centre line pylon. 2 x 500 lb. or 250 lb. bombs, depth charges, 8 x 60 lb. rockets, 12 x 25 lb. rockets, 45 gallon drop tanks, flares or markers under the wings.
Squadron Service 813, 827, 736, 738 and 759 Squadrons.
Notes An enormous aircraft with little appeal to its pilots, the Firebrand was conceived in 1939 as a carrier borne interceptor. Its development spanned the war years and it saw limited service post war as a strike aircraft armed with torpedo or bombs. It was by then totally outclassed by contemporary fighters. 220 delivered, mostly TF4s. They were replaced in service by Wyverns.

27 February 1942	First prototype (DD804) flew
February 1943	Second prototype (DD810) carried out deck landing trials on HMS ILLUSTRIOUS
September 1945	First Squadron, 813, formed
June 1946	Firebrands of 813 in Victory Flypast over London
April 1947	813 re-equipped with TF5s
1952	827 Squadron formed for HMS EAGLE
1953	Last Firebrands retired

FIREBRAND TF4 in flight showing the colour scheme in use in 1946.

BLACKBURN BUCCANEER

Variants S1 S2
Role Low level strike
Details are for S2
Engine 2 x 11,100 lb. thrust Rolls Royce Spey 101 turbojets
Span 44′0″ **Length** 63′5″ **Max Weight** 62,000 lbs.
Max Speed Mach 0.85 **Crew** Pilot and Observer
Armament Internal bomb bay with rotating door capable of carrying a nuclear store, 4 x 1000 lb. or 500 lb. bombs, a camera reconnaissance pack or 440 gallon long range tank. 4 wing hardpoints each stressed to 3000 lb. capable of carrying Bullpup, Martel or Sidewinder missiles, 1000 lb. or 500 lb. bombs, 2″ rocket pods or Lepus flares. Inboard hardpoints "plumbed" for drop tanks or a Flight Refuelling Ltd. pack enabling the aircraft to act as an air to air tanker.
Squadron Service 800, 801, 803, 809, 700Z, 700B and 736 Squadrons
Notes The FAA's extensive experience in Korea led to the far sighted specification NA39 for the World's first specialised low level strike aircraft. The resulting Buccaneer was arguably the best aircraft ever procured for the RN and it proved outstanding in its intended role capable of long range at high speed at sea level. Politics dogged the aircraft however, cancellation of the new generation of carriers in 1966 relegated it to use from modernised small carriers of World War II vintage which restricted the outstanding potential of the design. The only foreign sale was to South Africa. A total of 124 production Buccaneers were delivered to the RN, some of which were passed to the RAF with the demise of the conventional carrier force.

July 1955	Development batch of 20 Buccaneers ordered
30 April 1958	First prototype (XK486) flew
June 1959	Deck landing trials on HMS VICTORIOUS
March 1961	700Z IFTU formed at RNAS LOSSIEMOUTH
17 May 1963	Pre-production S2 (XK526) a converted S1 flew
December 1963	Last S1 (XN973) delivered
6 June 1964	First production S2 (XN974) flew
April 1965	700B IFTU formed at RNAS LOSSIEMOUTH
December 1968	Last production Buccaneer (XV869) delivered to RN
December 1978	The last Squadron, 809, disbanded after HMS ARK ROYAL paid off

2 Buccaneers a prototype (XK488) and an S1 (XN967) are on display at the FAA Museum.

BUCCANEER S2 of 800 squadron from HMS EAGLE. Note the open bomb bay with 4 × 1000lb. bombs inside with 4 further bombs under the wings.

BRITISH AEROSPACE SEA HARRIER

Variants FRS 1
Role Short or vertical take off and landing fighter, reconnaissance and strike.
Engine 1 x 21,500 lb. thrust Rolls Royce Pegasus 104
Span 25′3″ **Length** 47′7″ **Max Weight** 26,200 lbs.
Max Speed Mach 1.2 **Crew** Pilot
Armament 2 x 30 mm Aden cannons with 120 rounds per gun in detachable pods, one on either side of the lower fuselage. 1 fuselage centreline and 4 underwing hardpoints. The inner wing points are capable of carrying 2000 lb. of stores and are plumbed for drop tanks. The other positions can carry 1000 lb. Possible loads include 1000 lb, 500 lb. or practice bombs, 2″ rocket pods, BL755 cluster bombs, Lepus flares, Sidewinder air to air missiles or 100 gallon drop tanks. The Sea Eagle air to surface missile is in development for this aircraft for service in the mid 1980s. A single F95 camera is mounted obliquely in the nose
Squadron Service 800, 801, 809, 899 and 700A Squadrons
Notes The Sea Harrier is an extremely versatile combat aircraft and represents excellent value for money. Its ancestry can be traced back through the RAF Harrier to the P1127 which first flew in 1960. The retaking of the Falkland Islands in 1982 would not have been possible without the air cover given to the Task Force by 800 and 801 Squadrons embarked in HM Ships HERMES and INVINCIBLE together with reinforcements of Aircraft and Men from 899, the Headquarters Squadron from RNAS YEOVILTON. It also proved possible to form a fourth Squadron, 809, with reserve aircraft and crews soon after the start of the conflict. The conflict confirmed what had been suspected from exercises that the Sea Harrier in skilled hands is without equal in air combat. It must now have notable export potential. It has been exported to India already and a number of other navies are showing keen interest. A much improved version is on the drawing board to be known as the FRS 2. It is to have the new BLUE VIXEN pulse doppler radar and provision for the Anglo/US AMRAAM MISSILE. When it flies in the late 1980's it will be the most potent single seat fighter in the western world

1971	Design studies started on a navalised Harrier
May 1975	Sea Harrier ordered into production
9 January 1978	First aircraft (XZ450) flew
19 September 1979	700A IFTU formed at RNAS YEOVILTON
31 March 1980	800 Squadron commissioned at RNAS YEOVILTON
22 May 1980	700A recommissioned as 899 Squadron
26 February 1981	801 Squadron commissioned at RNAS YEOVILTON
April 1982	809 Squadron formed at RNAS YEOVILTON

A SEA HARRIER prepares for take off aboard HMS ARK ROYAL.

CHANCE VOUGHT CORSAIR

Variants F1 F4
Role Fighter or fighter bomber
Details are for F4
Engine 1 x 2,250 hp Pratt and Whitney Double Wasp R-2800-8
Span 39′8″ **Length** 33′4″ **Max Weight** 12,100 lbs.
Max Speed 365 knots **Crew** Pilot
Armament 4 x 0.5″ Browning machine guns in wings. Hardpoints under the inboard wing sections for up to 2 x 1000 lb. or 500 lb. bombs or 100 gallon drop tanks
Squadron Service 1831, 1846, 1850 and 1851 Squadrons
Notes The RN received 1,977 Corsairs from the USA under Lend/Lease arrangements but most of these were destroyed or returned shortly after VJ Day since they couldn't be purchased outright. Four Squadrons were retained however, since they were embarked in light fleet carriers in the Far East which could not easily be re-equipped with British types. The Corsair was one of the classic piston engined fighters and although soon outclassed by the Sea Fury in the RN, it continued in service with the US and French Navies until the late 1950s

August 1945	Rapid disposal of Corsair force
January 1946	Light Fleet Carriers GLORY, COLOSSUS, VENERABLE and VENGEANCE retained Corsair squadrons temporarily
August 1946	1851, the last Corsair Squadron, disbanded

A Corsair F4 (KD431) can be seen in the FAA Museum

CORSAIR 4 outside the Fleet Air Arm Museum. (It is now on display inside.)

ROYAL NAVY
KD 431
E2-M

DE HAVILLAND SEA MOSQUITO

Variants TR33 TR37 TT39 and various ex RAF Mosquitoes used in a variety of training roles
Role Long range strike
Details for TR33
Engine 2 x 1640 hp Rolls Royce Merlin 25
Span 54′2″ **Length** 42′3″ **Max Weight** 22,500 lbs.
Max Speed 380 knots **Crew** Pilot and Observer
Armament 4 x 20 mm cannon in fuselage. 1 x external 18″ torpedo or 2 x 500 lb. bombs in rear bomb bay. Provision for 2 x 500 lb. bombs, up to 8 x 60 lb. rockets or drop tanks under wings
Squadron Service 811, 703, 728, 762, 771, 772, 778 and 790 Squadrons and various Station Flights
Notes A derivative of the famous RAF Wartime bomber, many of which were used by the Fleet Requirements Units. 50 new TR33s were built for the RN followed by 6 of the improved TR37s intended for the strike role from carriers with torpedoes or bombs

25 March 1944	Mosquito 6 piloted by Lt Cdr E M Brown RN landed on HMS INDEFATIGABLE. First twin engined aircraft to land on a British Carrier
Late 1945	Production of Sea Mosquito commenced
August 1946	811 Squadron formed with TR33s at RNAS FORD
July 1947	811 Squadron disbanded at RNAS BRAWDY

The remaining Sea Mosquitoes were used for second line duties until they were scrapped in the early 1950s. The TR37 never saw front line service

A brand new SEA MOSQUITO TR33 pictured shortly after completion in 1946.

DE HAVILLAND SEA HORNET

Variants F20 NF21 PR22
Role Fighter, night fighter and photographic reconnaissance
Details are for NF21
Engine 2 x 2030 hp Rolls Royce Merlin 134/135
Span 45′0″ **Length** 37′0″ **Max Weight** 19,530 lbs.
Max Speed 400 knots **Crew** Pilot and Observer (other versions Pilot only)
Armament 4 x 20 mm cannon in nose. Provision underwing for up to 8 x 60 lb. rockets or 2 x 500 lb. or 1000 lb. bombs
Squadron Service 801, 806, 809, 703, 728, 736, 738, 739, 762, 771, 778, 787 and 792 Squadrons. Fleet Requirements Units at Hurn and St Davids
Notes Evolved from the RAF's Hornet long range fighter. Saw limited service in the late 1940s and early 1950s. Main use was from shore bases since it proved difficult to deploy to all but the largest carriers and even then special barriers were required since the Pilot, with no engine in front of him, was more vulnerable in the event of a bad landing. The NF21 was extensively redesigned with AI radar in the nose and an observer's cockpit. From 1949 to 1954 it was the Fleet's only front line night fighter and it served with only one squadron, 809, which detached flights to various carriers during exercises. The PR22 was fitted with 2 x F52 cameras for day or 1 x K19B camera for night work. Without armament it was the fastest of the 3 versions. In all the RN received 198 Sea Hornets. Many were used in the 1950s to test catapults, being fired off without the outer wing panels as deadweights which were not recovered

19 April 1945	First prototype (PX212) flew
1 June 1947	801 Squadron re-formed with Sea Hornets at RNAS FORD
1948	806 Squadron toured USA and Canada with Sea Hornets, Sea Furies and a Sea Vampire
9 July 1946	Prototype NF21 (PX230) flew
20 January 1949	809 Squadron re-formed with NF21s at RNAS CULDROSE
1951	801 Sea Hornets replaced by Sea Furies
1954	809 Sea Hornets replaced by Sea Venoms

SEA HORNET Nf21s ranged on HMS EAGLE with ATTACKERS and FIREFLIES in background.

DE HAVILLAND SEA VAMPIRE

Variants F20 F21 T22
Role Fighter, pilot trainer
Details are for F20
Engine 1 x 3000 lb. thrust de Havilland Goblin 2
Span 38′0″ **Length** 30′9″ **Max Weight** 12,660 lbs.
Max Speed 500 knots **Crew** Pilot
Armament 4 x 20 mm cannon in nose
Squadron Service 806, 700, 702, 703, 736, 738, 749, 759, 764, 771, 778, 781 and 787 Squadrons. Various Station Flights
Notes A navalised version of the RAF's Vampire FB5. The RN's first generation of jet fighter pilots flew it, but it only saw limited front line service due to fears that the slow acceleration of the engine would make deck operations dangerous. Two aircraft, VG701 and VT803 were built to test a rubberised deck surface intended to allow undercarriageless landings. They were designated F21s and carried out trials in HMS WARRIOR in 1949. These showed that such landings were possible but the idea found no practical application in the Fleet

3 December 1945	A modified Vampire 1 (LZ551) piloted by Lt Cdr E M Brown RN landed on HMS OCEAN, the first such landing by a pure jet aircraft in the world
October 1948	First production Sea Vampire (VV136) flew
June 1949	Last of 18 Sea Vampires (VV165) delivered
15 June 1953	Sea Vampire F20 flown by Rear Admiral W T Couchman, Flag Officer Flying Training, led the Coronation Review Flypast at Spithead

T22s equipped a number of second line squadrons for various duties in the 1950s and survived in several station flights well into the 1960s.
LZ551 and a T22 (XA129) are preserved in the FAA Museum

The prototype SEA VAMPIRE, LZ551 seconds after landing on HMS OCEAN.

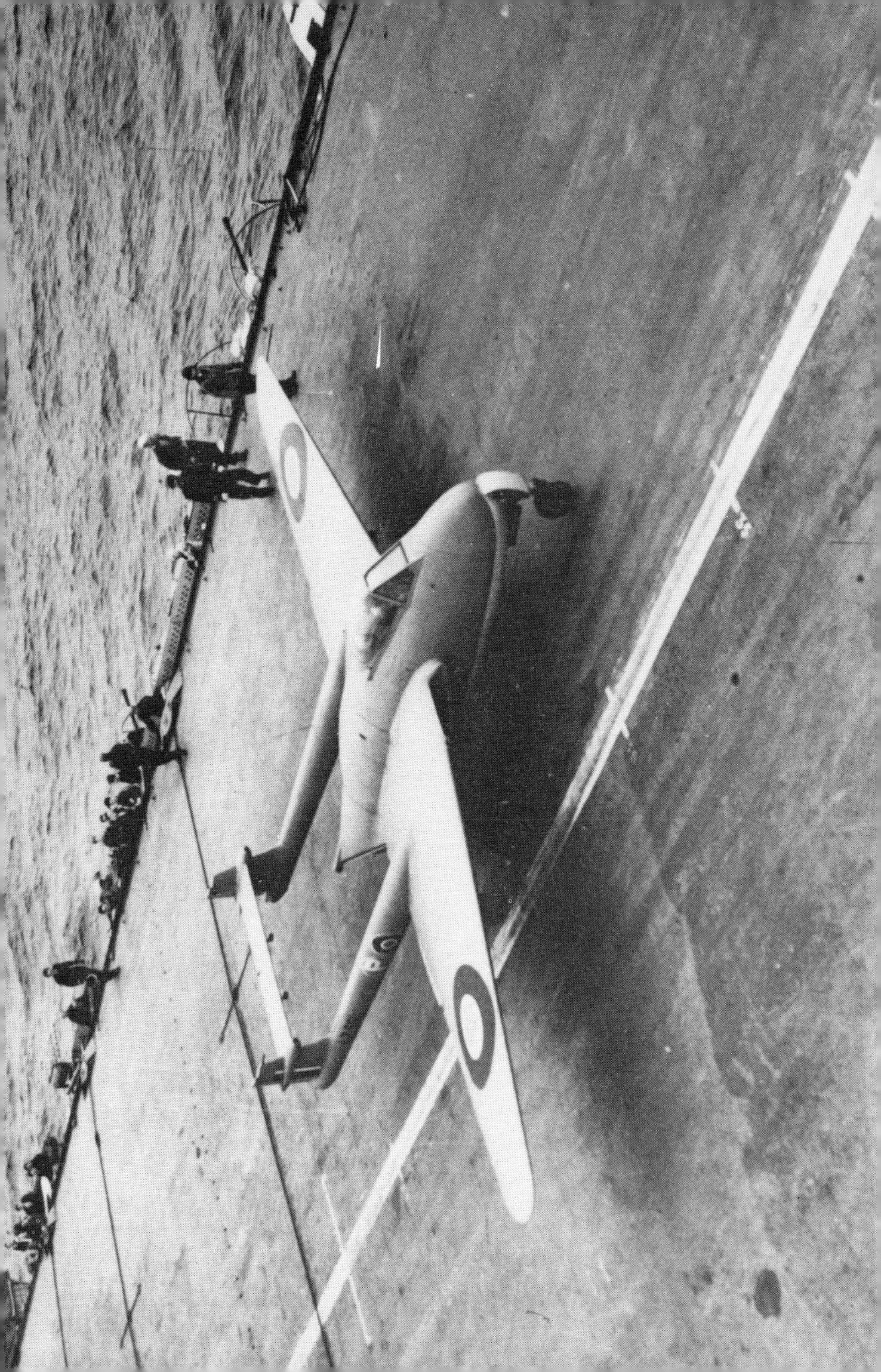

DE HAVILLAND SEA VENOM

Variants FAW20 FAW 21 FAW 22
Role Night and all weather fighter
Details are for FAW22
Engine 1 x 5300 lb. thrust de Havilland Ghost 105
Span 42′10″ **Length** 36′8″ **Max Weight** 15,000 lbs.
Max Speed 537 knots **Crew** Pilot and Observer
Armament 4 x 20 mm cannon in nose. Underwing provision for 2 x 500 lb. bombs or 8 x 60 lb. rockets. A small number of FAW22s modified to take Firestreak air to air missiles
Squadron Service 809, 831, 890, 891, 892, 893, 894, 895, 736, 738, 750 and 766 Squadrons and The Aircraft Direction Training Unit RNAS YEOVILTON
Notes The Sea Venom replaced the Sea Hornet as the standard night fighter but saw much more extensive service. A development of the RAF Venom NF2, it suffered many teething troubles not least being the difficulty experienced by pilots in bailing out of early aircraft which had no ejection seats. These were overcome with the FAW21 and 22 which were successful. Sea Venoms of 809, 891, 893, 894 and 895 Squadrons embarked in HM Ships EAGLE, ALBION and BULWARK played a prominent part in the SUEZ operation in November 1956 flying mainly in support of the Army ashore. In all the RN received 256

9 July 1951	First prototype (WK376) commenced carrier trials on HMS ILLUSTRIOUS
27 March 1953	First FAW20 (WM500) flew
20 March 1954	890, the first Squadron formed with FAW20s at RNAS YEOVILTON
22 April 1954	First FAW21 (WM568) flew
1958	FAW22s of 893 Squadron embarked in HMS VICTORIOUS carried out the RN's first front line air to air missile firings off Malta scoring 80% hits
24 October 1960	766 re-equipped with Sea Vixens for pilot conversion
6 October 1970	Last Sea Venom retired from Air Work FRU at RNAS YEOVILTON

Many have found their way into museums around the country and one (WW138) can be seen at the FAA Museum

SEA VENOM FAW21 of 890 squadron.

ROYAL NAVY
WM223

DE HAVILLAND SEA VIXEN

Variants FAW1 FAW2
Role Night and all weather fighter
Details are for FAW2
Engine 2 x 11,250 lb. thrust Rolls Royce Avon 208
Span 50′0″ **Length** 53′6½″ **Max Weight** 46,750 lbs.
Max Speed 610 knots **Crew** Pilot and Observer
Armament Provision on 6 underwing hardpoints for Firestreak or Red Top air to air missiles (FAW1 Firestreak only), 2″ rocket pods, 1000 lb. or 500 lb. bombs or 3″ rockets with "Gloworm" illuminant heads. 200 gallon drop tanks, LP air starter pods or an air refuelling pod on the outboard hardpoints only. A luggage pod could also be carried
Squadron Service 890, 892, 893, 899, 700Y and 766 Squadrons and FRADU at RNAS YEOVILTON
Notes Developed from the DH110 originally intended to meet both RN and RAF specifications, the Sea Vixen was the first FAA fighter with no gun armament. With heat seeking air to air missiles, AI18 radar and a vastly greater performance than the Sea Venom, it gave Fleet Fighter Squadrons a formidable multi-role capability throughout the 1960s. 143 Sea Vixens were built, including 67 that were converted from FAW1 to FAW2 standard

26 September 1951	Prototype DH110 (WG236) flew
5 April 1956	First navalised prototype (XF828) made first arrested landing on HMS ARK ROYAL
20 March 1957	First production FAW1 (XJ474) flew
November 1958	700Y IFTU formed at RNAS YEOVILTON
2 July 1959	892, the first operational squadron, formed at RNAS YEOVILTON
1 June 1962	First prototype FAW2 (XN684) flew
8 March 1963	First production FAW2 (XP919) flew
September 1968	892 Squadron formed "Simon's Sircus" display team for SBAC show at RAE Farnborough
February 1972	899, the last front line Sea Vixen Squadron, disbanded following the withdrawal of HMS EAGLE from service

An FAW1 (XJ481) and an FAW2 (XS590) can be seen at the FAA Museum

SEA VIXEN FAW1 of 893 Squadron about to be catapulted from HMS VICTORIOUS.

XN698
ROYAL NAVY
ROYAL NAVY
220
C

DOUGLAS SKYRAIDER

Variants AEW1
Role Airborne early warning
Engine 1 x 2700 hp Wright Cyclone R-3350-26WA
Span 50′0″ **Length** 38′10″ **Max Weight** 24,000 lbs.
Max Speed 305 knots **Crew** Pilot and 2 Observers
Armament nil
Squadron Service 849 and 778 Squadrons
Notes Supplied by the USN under the Mutual Defence Aid Programme, Skyraiders were fitted with the AN/APS 20 radar later fitted in a more advanced form to the Gannet AEW3. 20 Skyraiders were built for the RN at the Douglas Factory at El Segundo, California and 30 were refurbished USN aircraft. This variant was known as the AD4W in the USN. Since they were already in US service, Skyraiders did not go through the usual acceptance procedure apart from compatibility checks with RN catapults and arrester gear at RAE FARNBOROUGH. 778 Squadron was formed to work out RN AEW tactical doctrine and evaluate the electronic equipment under operational conditions. The USN operated the aircraft purely as an airborne radar set and even carried maintainers to transmit the best picture to the parent carrier. The RN, however, operated each aircraft as an autonomous unit with highly trained observers capable of interpreting the radar picture and using it to intercept air raids with fighters or to control strike aircraft onto their target. The Skyraider was a successful and popular aircraft. 849 Squadron deployed flights lettered A to E to all the carriers in commission through the 1950s. The type always suffered from a shortage of spares and a number had to be cannibalised at RNAS DONIBRISTLE to keep the remainder at sea

1 October 1951	778 Squadron commissioned at RNAS CULDROSE
9 November 1951	First 4 aircraft delivered by sea for 778 Squadron
7 July 1952	778 disbanded and 849 commissioned at RNAS CULDROSE
3 November 1952	849A, the first operational flight, formed
19 February 1953	13 further aircraft delivered in HMS PERSEUS
1956	Last aircraft delivered
December 1960	Last aircraft retired

Two examples survive, WT121 in the FAA Museum and WV106 at RNAS CULDROSE

SKYRAIDER of 849 'B' flight ready for free take off from HMS ARK ROYAL.

421
ROYAL N

FAIREY BARRACUDA

Variants TBR3 AS3 TBR5
Role Torpedo, bomber, reconnaissance and anti-submarine search or strike aircraft
Details are for AS3
Engine 1 x 1640 hp Rolls Royce Merlin 32
Span 49′2″ **Length** 39′9″ **Max Weight** 14,250 lbs.
Max Speed 315 knots **Crew** Pilot, Observer and Telegraphist Air Gunner
Armament 1 x 1572 lb. torpedo, 4 x 250 lb. depth charges or up to 6 x 250 lb. bombs
Squadron Service 815, 821, 860, 700, 744, 750, 781 and 783 Squadrons
Notes The Barracuda saw extensive service in all theatres during World War II, but with the rapid run down of the RN after VJ day all front line Barracuda Squadrons were disbanded by early 1946. After the return or destruction of all US Lend/Lease equipment however, the FAA found itself short of front line aircraft in the austere post war years. So somewhat surprisingly 815 Squadron reformed with AS3s brought out of storage in December 1947. This was the only front line Squadron to use the type post war but a number of Barracudas saw service in second line squadrons including a small batch of TBR5s with Griffon engines and improved performance

22 November 1945	The first TBR5 (RK530) flew
27 October 1947	The last Barracuda (RK574) delivered to the RN
December 1947	815 Squadron reformed with AS3s at RNAS EGLINTON
May 1953	Barracudas replaced by Grumman Avenger AS4s in 815 Squadron

The wreckage of a wartime TBR2 (DP872) is stored at the FAA Museum

BARRACUDA taking off from HMS INDOMITABLE.

FAIREY FIREFLY

Variants F1 NF2 FR4 FR5 AS4 AS5 AS6 AS7 T1 T2 T3 TT4 T7 U8 U9 and U10
Role Fighter reconnaissance, anti-submarine search or strike and a variety of training roles. U versions were pilotless target aircraft
Details are for FR4
Engine 1 x 2004 hp Rolls Royce Griffon 74
Span 41′0″ **Length** 37′0″ **Max Weight** 15,615 lbs.
Max Speed 370 knots **Crew** Pilot and Observer
Armament 4 x 20 mm cannon in wings with 160 rounds per gun. Provision for 2 x 1000 lb. or 500 lb. bombs, 8 x 25 lb. or 60 lb. rockets, mines, depth charges, flares or markers on underwing pylons
Squadron Service 805, 810, 812, 814, 816, 817, 820, 821, 822, 824, 825, 826, 827, 837, 847, 882, 1830, 1833, 1840, 1841, 1842, 1843, 1844, 700, 719, 728, 732, 736, 737, 744, 746, 750, 765, 766, 767, 771, 778, 780, 781, 782, 784, 792, 795 and 796 Squadrons. Various Station Flights
Notes The number of different variants and squadrons that used the Firefly after 1945 give testimony to the excellence of this aircraft. Popular with aircrew, the Firefly was the last of a long line of FAA 2 seat reconnaissance fighters and the last fighter built by Fairey Aviation. Together with Sea Furies, they bore the brunt of operations over Korea between 1950 and 1953 with 810, 812, 821, 825 and 827 Squadrons operating from HM Ships TRIUMPH, THESEUS, OCEAN and GLORY (plus 817 Squadron RAN from HMAS SYDNEY). Throughout, the Firefly maintained an admirable record of serviceability and effectiveness. 1702 were delivered to the RN, with others exported to Australia, Canada, Holland, Sweden, Ethiopia, Denmark and Thailand

22 December 1941	First prototype (Z1826) flew
25 May 1945	First production FR4 (TW687) delivered
23 November 1946	Last FR1 (DK570) delivered
15 June 1953	Firefly Squadrons formed the greater part of the Coronation Review Flypast with aircraft from 719, 737, 750, 766B, 771, 781, 796, 812, 814, 817 (RAN), 820, 824, 825, 826, 1830, 1840 and 1841 Squadrons
20 March 1956	The last Firefly delivered, a U8 (WP354)
1956	Firefly replacement by AS Gannets completed

A single Firefly FR5 (WB271) is maintained in flying condition by the Historic Aircraft Flight at RNAS YEOVILTON. An AS4 (VH127) can be seen in the FAA Museum

FIREFLY AS6 on the lift of HMS EAGLE.

FAIREY GANNET

Variants AS1 T2 AS4 T5 AS6
Role Anti-submarine search and strike, pilot and armament conversion trainer
Engine 1 x 2750 shp Armstrong Siddeley Double Mamba 101 Unit
Span 54′4″ **Length** 43′0″ **Max Weight** 23,700 lbs.
Max Speed 360 knots **Crew** Pilot, Observer and Aircrewman
Armament Large bomb bay capable of carrying variations of 81 gallon fuel tanks, 2 x Mk30 homing torpedoes, 1 x 2000 lb., 2 x 1000 lb. or 4 x 500 lb. bombs, 6 x depth charges, mines, flares or markers. Underwing provision for 16 x 3″ rockets with either 25 lb. or illuminant warheads
Squadron Service 810, 812, 814, 815, 816 (RAN), 817 (RAN), 820, 824, 825, 826, 831, 847, 849, 896, 1840, 1842, 700, 703X, 719, 737, 744, 771 and 796 Squadrons
Notes The FAA's first anti-submarine aircraft capable of combining the search and strike roles in a single sortie. The Gannet suffered a prolonged development period despite the award of "super priority" status during the Korean War. It was retired prematurely in 1960 due to the unexpectedly rapid development of the anti-submarine helicopter and the lack of space in RN carriers for both types. The observer was replaced by an instructor pilot in the T2 and T5 and the radar deleted although the weapon capability was retained Trainers could carry two passengers in the aircrewman's cockpit. Most Gannets went for storage and then scrap after Whirlwind 7 Helicopters replaced them. A few AS4s were refurbished in 1961 with new radar and electronics for service with 831 Electronic Warfare Squadron at RNAS CULDROSE. 5 others were converted to COD4 standard for carrier on board delivery of mail, stores and passengers to the Fleet at sea. A total of 298 (excluding AEW3) were delivered to the RN and the type was exported to Australia, Germany and Indonesia

12 August 1946 — Contract awarded for 2 Fairey type Q prototypes
19 September 1949 — First prototype (VR546) flew
19 June 1950 — First landing (VR546) on HMS ILLUSTRIOUS by Lt Cdr G R CALLINGHAM RN (first ever by a turboprop aircraft)
9 June 1953 — First production aircraft (WN339) flew
5 April 1954 — 703X Intensive Trials Flight formed at RNAS FORD
17 January 1955 — First Squadron, 826, formed for service in HMS EAGLE
February 1955 — First trainers sent to 737 Squadron at RNAS EGLINTON
12 March 1956 — First AS4 with uprated engines (XA410) flew
August 1956 — 824 Squadron first to be re-equipped with AS4s
July 1960 — 810 Squadron, last anti-submarine front line squadron disbanded

An AS4 (COD) (XA466) can be seen at the FAA Museum. A T5 (XT752) is held in storage for possible future use by the RN Historic Flight

GANNETS of 824 Squadron.

411
412
413
414
415
417
418
424
419
455
NAVY

FAIREY GANNET AEW

Variants AEW3
Role Airborne early warning and reconnaissance
Engine 1 x 3875 shp Armstrong Siddeley Double Mamba 112 (D8)
Span 54′4″ **Length** 44′0″ **Max Weight** 26,000 lbs.
Max Speed 280 knots **Crew** Pilot and 2 Observers
Armament Nil but an internal stores bay and 2 wing hardpoints could carry 100 gallon drop tanks, air starter units, flares, markers, rescue dinghy packs, etc.
Squadron Service 849 (HQ, A, B, C and D Flights) and 700G Squadrons
Notes 44 were built from 1958 onwards including a single prototype. The distinctive radome housed the AN/APS 20 search radar capable of detecting aircraft and ships at ranges considerably beyond sets mounted in ships of the Fleet. Observers were capable of controlling interceptions with fighters, directing strikes onto enemy ships and many other tasks. Continually updated, Gannets flew on until the RN paid off HMS ARK ROYAL, the last ship capable of operating them. The lack of long range radar warning and control capability since the demise of 849 Squadron was only too obvious in the Falklands Campaign

20 August 1958	First prototype (XJ440) flew
18 August 1959	700G Intensive Trials Squadron formed at RNAS CULDROSE CULDROSE
1 February 1960	AEW3 Gannets absorbed into 849 Squadron. Thence flights of 4 aircraft each served in HM Ships VICTORIOUS (A & B), CENTAUR (B), ARK ROYAL (B & C), EAGLE (D) and HERMES (A, B & C)
1965	849 HQ moved from RNAS CULDROSE to RNAS BRAWDY
November 1970	849 HQ moved again to RNAS LOSSIEMOUTH
February 1979	849B the last operational flight disbanded

Several AEW3s are retained in storage at RNAS CULDROSE for possible future use with the RN Historic Flight. A number are in museums around the country including XL503 in the FAA Museum

The Author in GANNET AEW3 043 of 849 'B' flight on HMS ARK ROYAL. A second GANNET in the background has been loaded onto the waist catapult.

ROYAL NAVY
044
NO STEP
RESCUE
LT HOBBS
043

GRUMMAN AVENGER

Variants TR3 AS4 AS5
Role Torpedo bomber and anti-submarine search and strike
Details are for AS4
Engine 1 x 1750 hp Wright Cyclone R-2600-20
Span 54′2″ **Length** 40′0″ **Max Weight** 16,760 lbs.
Max Speed 230 knots **Crew** Pilot, Observer and Telegraphist Air Gunner
Armament Up to 8 x 60 lb. rockets on underwing hardpoints. 1 x 0.5″ machine gun in power operated turret. Internal bomb bay capable of carrying a single torpedo, 2 x 1000 lb. or 4 x 500 lb. bombs
Squadron Service 814, 815, 820, 824, 828, 831, 1830, 1841, 1844, 703, 744 and 778 Squadrons. Various Ships & Station Flights.
Notes An effective and popular aircraft, the Avenger saw extensive service in World War II notably with the British Pacific Fleet. Like other Lend/Lease aircraft however it soon vanished, the last British squadron disbanding in 1946 although it remained in service in the USN. In 1953 it became apparent that the Firefly and Barracuda were obsolescent and the Gannet some way from operational service, so 100 Avenger AS aircraft were therefore given to the RN under the Mutual Defence Aid Programme to fill the gap in anti-submarine squadrons. The type augmented but did not wholly replace the Firefly and saw only limited service before the debut of the Gannet in 1955. Some served with RNVR air squadrons until their disbandment in 1957. A few were used for electronic warfare duties in 831 Squadron until the early 1960s. Modifications for the RN included much more comprehensive tactical control arrangements for the observer than those employed by the USN. Both the RN and RCN used Avengers as autonomous tactical units controlled by their crews unlike their US counterparts who relied on shipborne control

3 June 1946	828, last wartime Avenger squadron, disbanded
30 March 1953	First Avenger AS4s delivered in HMS PERSEUS
May 1953	815 Squadron recommissioned with Avengers
1955	Front line squadrons re-equipped with AS Gannets

A single Avenger (XB446) is preserved in the FAA Museum

AVENGER AS4 of 815 Squadron.

HAWKER SEA FURY

Variants F10 FB11 T20
Role Fighter, fighter bomber and conversion trainer
Details are for FB11
Engine 1 x 2480 hp Bristol Centaurus 18
Span 38′4¾″ **Length** 34′8″ **Max Weight** 14,650 lbs.
Max Speed 425 knots **Crew** Pilot
Armament 4 x 20 mm cannon in wings plus variations of 2 x 1000 lb. or 500 lb. bombs, up to 12 x 60 lb. rockets, 2 x 90 or 45 gallon drop tanks, mines, depth charges, flares or markers
Squadron Service 801, 802, 803, 804, 805, 807, 808 (RAN), 810, 811, 898, 1830, 1831, 1832, 1833, 1834, 1835, 1836, 1843, 703, 728, 736, 738, 759, 764, 766, 767, 771, 778, 781 and 796 Squadrons. Various Station Flights
Notes An excellent aircraft, well liked by its pilots, the Sea Fury was the standard single seat fleet fighter from 1947 to 1954 and the last powered by a piston engine. Together with the Firefly, it bore the brunt of the fighting in the Korean. War Sea Furies of 801, 802, 804, 805 (RAN), 807 and 808 (RAN) Squadrons were embarked in the Light Fleet Carriers OCEAN, GLORY, THESEUS and HMAS SYDNEY. 665 were delivered to the RN with others exported to Australia, Canada, Holland and Burma. A few were also used as target tugs in Germany. The Sea Fury was the first British built RN aircraft to have power folding wings. A number continued to fly on fleet requirements tasks with civilian pilots into the early 1960s

21 February 1945	First prototype (SR661) flew
October 1945	Deck landing trials by SR661 in HMS OCEAN
30 September 1946	First production aircraft (TF895) flew
August 1947	First Squadron, 807, formed at RNAS EGLINTON with F10s
May 1948	First Squadron, 802, formed with FB11s at RNAS EGLINTON
9 August 1952	MIG 15 jet shot down over Korea by Sea Fury FB11 (VR943) flown by Lt P Carmichael RN of 802 Squadron from HMS OCEAN
November 1952	Last production Sea Fury (WZ656) delivered
1954	Last Sea Furies replaced in front line service by Sea Hawks
1962	Last Sea Fury retired from Air Work FRU at Hurn

The first production FB11 (TF956) and a T20 (WG655) are preserved in flying condition by the RN Historic Flight at RNAS YEOVILTON. An FB11 (WJ231) is on display at the FAA Museum and an FB11 (VR930) is in storage

SEA FURIES onboard HMS OCEAN using the thrust of their propellors to help turn the ship in Grand Harbour, Malta.

WF624
148

HAWKER SEAHAWK

Variants F1 F2 FB3 FGA4 FB5 FGA6
Role Fighter, fighter bomber or ground attack
Details are for FGA6
Engine 1 x 5200 lb. Rolls Royce Nene 103
Span 39′0″ **Length** 39′10″ **Max Weight** 16,200 lbs.
Max Speed 520 knots **Crew** Pilot
Armament 4 x internal 20 mm cannon. Provision underwing for 10 x 3″ rockets or 2 x 100 gallon tanks on inboard pylons or up to 4 x 500 lb. bombs
Squadron Service 800, 801, 802, 803, 804, 806, 807, 810, 811, 895, 897, 898, 899, 1832, 1835, 1836, 700, 703, 736, 738, 764, 767 and 771 Squadrons. FRU at Hurn
Notes This attractive aircraft formed the backbone of the FAA's tactical fighter force for most of the 1950s. Sea Hawks of 800, 802, 804, 810, 897 and 899 Squadrons played a leading part in the Suez operation in 1956 embarked in HM Ships EAGLE, ALBION and BULWARK. A total of 434 were delivered to the RN with others exported to India, West Germany and Holland

February 1946	3 prototypes ordered
3 September 1948	First prototype (VP413) flew
November 1951	First production aircraft (WF143) flew
March 1953	First Squadron, 806, formed at RNAS BRAWDY
Early 1956	Last production Sea Hawk (XE490) delivered to RN
September 1957	5 red Sea Hawks of 738 Squadron formed part of SBAC Show at Farnborough
15 December 1960	Last front line Squadron, 806, disembarked from HMS ALBION to disband at RNAS BRAWDY

One FGA6 (WV908) is retained in flying condition at RNAS CULDROSE. One FGA6 (WV856) is on display at the FAA Museum and an F1 (WF219) and an FGA6 (XE340) are in storage

SEA HAWK FGA6's of 898 squadron. Note the later paint scheme on the nearer aircraft. The smoke marks on the port wings indicate that this has been a rocket firing sortie.

E
470
ROYAL NAVY
E
473
ROYAL NAVY
E
476

McDONNELL DOUGLAS PHANTOM

Variants FG1
Role Interceptor and ground attack fighter
Engine 2 x 12,250 lb. thrust reheated Rolls Royce RB 168 Spey Mk 201 turbofans
Span 38′4″ **Length** 57′7″ **Max Weight** 56,000 lbs.
Max Speed Mach 2.2 **Crew** Pilot and Observer
Armament Recessed stowage under fuselage for 4 Sparrow missiles. 4 underwing and 1 under fuselage hardpoints capable of carrying 3000 lb. of stores each. Underslung weapons included nuclear weapons, up to 4 Sidewinder missiles, 2 extra Sparrows, up to 3 x 2″ rocket pods or 3 x 1000 lb., 750 lb. or 500 lb. bombs per pylon. No gun was carried. Centreline and inboard wing hardpoints were plumbed for drop tanks
Squadron Service 892, 700P and 767 Squadrons
Notes The fastest and most capable fighter to serve with the RN to date and probably for all time. The Phantom was the standard USN fleet fighter throughout the 1960s and much of the 1970s. It was selected for the FAA in 1963 to replace the Sea Vixen following the failure of the Hawker P1154 multi-role V/STOL fighter to gain joint service acceptance. Originally an order of 200 was the aim, but this was whittled down to 28 following the political decision to run down the aircraft carrier force. Many of the cancelled airframes actually went to the RAF. Given the US designation F4K, the RN aircraft differed in having British engines and equipment, a folding nose radome, larger flaps, drooping ailerons, a slotted tailplane and a nose oleo (leg) that extended by 40″ to improve the take-off attitude. Changes forced by the need to operate the Phantom from smaller decks of British ships. A Phantom piloted by the CO of 892 Squadron, Lt Cdr B Davies RN, won the Daily Mail Transatlantic Air Race of May 1969 with a record crossing time of 4 hours 46 minutes 57 seconds

27 June 1966	First prototype (XT595) flew in USA
29 April 1968	First Phantoms delivered to RNAS YEOVILTON
30 April 1968	700P Intensive Trials Unit formed at RNAS YEOVILTON
14 January 1969	767 Training Squadron commissioned at RNAS YEOVILTON
31 March 1969	892 Squadron commissioned at RNAS YEOVILTON
Autumn 1969	892 embarked in USS SARATOGA in Mediterranean
12 June 1970	892 embarked in HMS ARK ROYAL
1972	767 disbanded. 892 Squadron's shore base transferred from RNAS YEOVILTON to RAF LEUCHARS as part of the run down of RN Air Stations
December 1978	892 disbanded following the paying off for disposal of HMS ARK ROYAL, the only British ship to operate the type. The remaining aircraft were handed over to the RAF

PHANTON FG1 of 892 Squadron seconds after leaving the waist catapault of HMS ARK ROYAL.

001
ROYAL NAVY
R

SIKORSKY S55 (WHIRLWIND)

Variants HAR21 HAS22
Role Search and rescue, utility and anti-submarine helicopter
Details are as for the Westland Whirlwind except for the engine
Engine HAR21 1 x 600 hp Pratt and Whitney Wasp R-1340-40
HAS22 1 x 700 hp Wright Cyclone R-1300-3
Armament Nil
Squadron Service 845, 848 and 781 Squadrons
Notes Prior to the availability of the licence built Westland Whirlwind, 25 Sikorsky Whirlwinds were made available in 1952 under the MDAP to give the RN helicopter experience. 10 were to HAR21 standard and 15 to HAS22 standard. The 10 HAR21s were used to equip the FAA's first operational helicopter squadron, 848, in November 1952. In March 1953 these went into action in Malaya and saw extensive service against the communist insurgents. The majority of HAS22s equipped 845 Squadron which became operational in March 1954 and was used to evaluate the concept of the anti-submarine helicopter equipped with dipping sonar. These trials proved highly successful and led to the dominance of helicopter ASW tactics from 1960 onwards. Sikorsky Whirlwinds were replaced in front line squadrons by Westland built examples but some soldiered on in utility duties with 781 Squadron until as late as 1969

WHIRLWIND HAR21 winching officers from the casing of a submarine.

ROYAL NAVY
ROYAL NAVY

SUPERMARINE SEAFIRE

Variants F15 F17 F45 F46 FR47
Role Fighter, fighter reconnaissance
Details are for FR47
Engine 1 x 2375 hp Rolls Royce Griffon 85
Span 36′11″ **Length** 34′4″ **Max Weight** 11,615 lbs.
Max Speed 400 knots **Crew** Pilot
Armament 4 x 20 mm cannon in wings. 8 x 60 lb. rockets or up to 2 x 500 lb. bombs underwing. 1 x 500 lb. bomb on centreline. Provision underwing for 90 gallon fuel tanks
Squadron Service 800, 802, 803, 804, 805, 806, 1830, 1831, 1832, 736, 738, 759, 764, 767, 771, 778 and 781 Squadrons
Notes Wartime Seafires had Merlin engines and disappeared rapidly after VJ Day. The Griffon engined Seafires were more capable aircraft with increased internal fuel and an improved arrester hook. They were the backbone of the RN fighter squadrons in the late 1940s after all the Lend/Lease aircraft had gone. The marks 45 and 46 were not fully deck capable. The FR47 was however and proved to be a potent general purpose aircraft—a far cry from the first Spitfire from which it was a direct descendent. FR47s of 800 Squadron embarked in HMS TRIUMPH saw action in 1949 against communist guerillas in Malaya and in the Korean War through 1950. They were replaced in front line squadrons by Sea Furies and Attackers. The RN received 780 Griffon engined Seafires. Despite its shortcomings as a deck landing aircraft, the Seafire gave 13 years valuable service in peace and war

May 1945	802 Squadron commissioned with F15s at RNAS ARBROATH
July 1947	1832 RNVR Squadron commissioned with F46s at RNAS CULHAM
February 1948	804 Squadron commissioned with FR47s at RNAS FORD
November 1954	764, the last Seafire Squadron in the RN gave up its last aircraft at RNAS YEOVILTON

A single example (SX137) is preserved in the FAA Museum

SEAFIRE FR47's of 800 squadron disembarked with the remainder of their Air Group (FIREFLIES and a SEA OTTER). One or two aircraft retain the old 1940's colour scheme.

SUPERMARINE ATTACKER

Variants F1 FB1 FB2
Role Fighter, fighter bomber
Details are for F1
Engine 1 x 5,100 lb. thrust Rolls Royce Nene 3
Span 36′11″ **Length** 37′6″ **Max Weight** 11,500 lbs.
Max Speed 520 knots **Crew** Pilot
Armament 4 x 20 mm Hispano cannon in wings. (FB2 had provision for a 250 gallon drop tank below fuselage and up to 8 x 60 lb. rockets or 2 x 1000 lb. bombs under wings.)
Squadron Service 800, 803, 890, 1831, 1832, 1833, 1834, 1835, 702, 736, 738, 767, 771, 778 and 787 Squadrons
Notes The Attacker was the first jet fighter to equip a FAA front line squadron. It was conservative in design employing the laminar flow wing intended for the Spiteful/Seafang piston engine fighters and thus it was descended directly from the Spitfire series. A difficult aircraft to deck land due to its awkward tail-wheel undercarriage. It was not a success in service and was replaced in regular squadrons by the Seahawk as soon as it was available, although a number did remain with the RNR air squadrons until they disbanded. The development was drawn out over a number of years while the Admiralty hesitated over the decision of whether to take the plunge and form jet air groups with their new and as yet unanswered problems in carrier launch and recovery, or to stay a little longer with the piston engined types that were at their zenith in the late 1940s. The Attacker was the only jet ever to see service with a tail wheel undercarriage. The FAA received a total of 145

17 June 1947	First navalised prototype (TS413) flew
October 1947	Carrier trials on HMS ILLUSTRIOUS by TS413
November 1949	Production contracts placed
April 1950	First production aircraft (WA469) flew
22 August 1951	First Squadron, 800, commissioned at RNAS FORD
May 1954	Attackers replaced by Sea Hawks in front line squadrons
May 1955	1831 RNR Squadron received Attackers
August 1957	All Attackers struck off charge after RNR air squadrons disbanded

One Attacker (WA473) is on display in the FAA Museum

ATTACKER F1 in flight.

SUPERMARINE SCIMITAR

Variants F1
Role Fighter, reconnaissance and strike
Engine 2 x 11,250 lb. thrust Rolls Royce Avon 202 turbojets
Span 37′2″ **Length** 55′4″ **Max Weight** 40,000 lbs.
Max Speed 625 knots **Crew** Pilot
Armament 4 x 30 mm Aden guns in fuselage. Four underwing hardpoints each capable of carrying one of the following:- A tactical nuclear weapon, Sidewinder air to air or Bullpup air to surface missile, 2″ rocket pod, 3″ rocket, 500 lb. or 1000 lb. bomb. 250 gallon drop tanks could be carried on the inboard pylons and 100 gallon drop tanks on the outboard pylons. An air to air refuelling pod could be carried
Squadron Service 800, 800B, 803, 804, 807, 703X and 736 Squadrons. Airwork manned Fleet Requirements Unit at Hurn Airport Bournemouth
Notes The Scimitar was an odd mixture. It was the first RN aircraft with swept wings, the first RN aircraft to break the sound barrier in a shallow dive and the first capable of carrying a tactical nuclear weapon. But it was also the last RN fighter to have no fire control radar, no sophisticated navigation system and indeed no space for an observer. Its development spanned the 1950s and it represented a number of compromises all of which forced up the basic weight. It was the first British service aircraft to use blown flaps to reduce the safe approach speed and the first to have area ruling applied in the fuselage design. It will be remembered with affection by some pilots but was disliked by engineers who found it a hard aircraft to maintain. Scimitars leaked fuel like young puppies when parked on the flight deck and had to be constantly supplied with drip trays and even dustbins. They were rapidly replaced in service by the much more capable Buccaneer. Scimitars found a last role in 800B Squadron acting as air to air refuelling tankers for Buccaneers in HMS EAGLE. An alternative nose cone containing a camera could be fitted for the reconnaissance role. 76 were delivered to the RN, a further 24 being cancelled due to the success of the more capable second generation jets such as the Buccaneer and Sea Vixen

20 January 1956	First prototype (WT854) flew
11 January 1957	First production aircraft (XD212) flew
August 1957	703X Trials Flight formed at RNAS FORD
June 1958	First Squadron, 803, commissioned at RNAS LOSSIEMOUTH
October 1966	800B the last Scimitar squadron disbanded

Scimitars were used by the civilian manned FRU at Hurn until the early 1970s
2 Scimitars survive today (XD317 and XD220), both in the FAA Museum

SCIMITARS rehearsing for an air display.

WESTLAND WYVERN

Variants S4 (TF1 TF2 T3 development only)
Role Torpedo strike fighter
Engine 1 x 4,110 hp Armstrong Siddeley Python ASP3 turboprop
Span 44′0″ . **Length** 42′3″ **Max Weight** 24,500 lbs.
Max Speed 330 knots **Crew** Pilot
Armament 4 x 20 mm Hispano cannon in wings. Hardpoints for a single torpedo, 3 x 1000 lb. or 500 lb. bombs or 8 x 3″ or 16 x 2″ unguided rockets
Squadron Service 813, 827, 830, 831, 700, 703, 764 and 787 Squadrons
Notes The Wyvern replaced the obsolete Firebrand after an amazing 7 years of development flying. What had seemed a good idea in 1945 proved extremely difficult to translate into hardware and 3 different engines were tried. The only mark to see service, the S4, was never a success and its duties were eventually undertaken by jet fighters after 1958. One Squadron, 830, saw action from HMS EAGLE in the Suez intervention in 1956. A single example of the T3, a 2 seat trainer, was built but never saw service. 7 Wyvern TF2s were delivered as S4s and 90 S4s were built as such. The type is remembered for excessive losses and some horrific deck landing accidents. All remaining S4s were scrapped in 1959

12 December 1946	First Wyvern (TS371) flew
18 January 1949	First turboprop powered Wyvern (VP120) flew with a Rolls Royce Clyde engine
May 1951	First S4 (VZ745) flew
May 1953	Wyverns replaced Firebrands in 813 Squadron at RNAS FORD
March 1958	813, by then the last Wyvern Squadron, disbanded at RNAS FORD

A single TF1 development airframe (VR137) survives in the FAA Museum. It has a Rolls Royce Eagle piston engine

WYVERN S4 firing 3″ rockets with 60 lb warheads.

WYVERN S4 of 813 Squadron on board HMS EAGLE

GANNET AS4

SEAHAWK of 806 Squadron

SEA VENOM of 894 Squadron

WESSEX HAS 3 of 737 Squadron

WASP HAS 1 of 703 Squadron a split second after firing an AS12 guided missile

GANNET AEW 3 of 849 B Flight — HMS ARK ROYAL

SCIMITAR F Mk 1 of 803 Squadron

BUCCANEER S2 of 809 Squadron, seconds before catching a wire on board HMS ARK ROYAL

PHANTOM FG1 of 892 Squadron leaves the waist catapult of HMS ARK ROYAL

WYVERN S4 of 831 squadron being catapulted from HMS ARK ROYAL.

WESTLAND WHIRLWIND

Variants HAR1 HAR3 HAR5 HAS7 HAR9
Role Anti-submarine search or strike, commando assault, search and rescue helicopter
Details are for HAS7
Engine 1 x 750 hp Alvis Leonides Major
Rotor Diameter 53′0″ **Length** 41′8½″ **Max Weight** 7,800 lbs.
Max Speed 90 knots **Crew** 1 or 2 Pilots, Observer in HAS version and up to 8 seats in HAR versions
Armaments HAR versions nil. HAS7 had provision for a single Mk 30 homing torpedo in a recess in the fuselage bottom when in the strike role
Squadron Service 814, 815, 820, 824, 845, 846, 847, 848, 705, 737, 771 and 781 Squadrons. SAR Flights at RN Air Stations
Notes The Sikorsky S55 helicopter allocated to the RN by the US in 1952 under the Mutual Defence Aid Plan, proved so successful that a licence built version, to be known as the Whirlwind, was ordered for the FAA in 1953. A total of 37 were built of the various HAR models, the HAR5 being the first with a British engine. These were followed by a production run of 120 HAS7 models equipped with dipping sonar or provision for a torpedo, both could not be carried simultaneously. The Whirlwind began to replace the Gannet in AS Squadrons in 1957 but suffered a number of teething troubles especially with regard to the engine and transmission. It did not, therefore, become the standard AS aircraft until 1960 by which time it was already obsolescent and within sight of replacement by the very much more capable Wessex. In 1956, Whirlwinds of 845 Squadron operating from HMS OCEAN landed men ashore from 45 Commando RM during the Suez landings—the first heliborne assault in history. This concept was taken up and from 1960 onwards, Whirlwinds equipped specialist commando assault squadrons in the converted Carriers BULWARK and ALBION. An unloved and unremarkable machine, the Whirlwind laid the foundation of the RN's expanding helicopter force in the early 1960s. Whirlwinds of 705 Squadron trained pilots to "Wings" standard for many years. A few HAS7 airframes were re-engined with a single Rolls Royce Gnome turbine engine from 1966 onwards for use in SAR Flights and were designated HAR9

15 August 1953	First HAR1 (XA862) flew
17 October 1956	First HAS7 (XG589) flew
June 1957	700 Squadron's evaluation of HAS7 commenced
August 1957	845 re-equipped, the first Squadron with HAS7s
August 1975	Last HAS7 retired from training role
1977	Last HAR9 retired from SAR role

An HAR1 (XA862) can be seen in the FAA Museum. Two HAR3s (XG574 and XJ402) and an HAS7 (XG594) are held in storage

WHIRLWIND HAR3 operating from HMS WARRIOR during Christmas Island tests.

ROYAL NAVY
995
XG588
BEWARE OF TAIL ROTOR
HMS WARRIOR
ROYAL NAVY
993
J

WESTLAND WESSEX

Variants HAS1 HAS3 HU5
Role Anti-submarine search and strike, commando assault and search and rescue helicopter
Details are for the HAS3
Engine 1 x 1600 shp Napier Gazelle 165 free power turbine
Rotor Diameter 56′0″ **Length** 65′10″ **Max Weight** 13,600 lbs.
Max Speed 120 knots **Crew** 1 or 2 Pilots, Aircrewman and up to 12 Passengers
Armament Detachable pylons could carry 2 x 7.62mm machine guns, 2 x 2″ rocket pods or up to 4 x SS11 or 2 x AS12 wire guided missiles. Hardpoints in fuselage sides could carry Mk11 depth charges, Mk44 or 46 homing torpedoes or 98 gallon drop tanks. Further 7.62mm machine guns could be mounted on pintles in the cabin door and rear windows
Squadron Service 814, 815, 819, 820, 824, 826, 829, 845, 846, 847, 848, 700H,700V, 706, 707, 737, 771, 772 and 781 Squadrons. Numerous carrier and air station SAR flights
Notes The Wessex has served the RN for 21 years. It was the world's first front line helicopter powered by a free power gas turbine. It was also the first ASW helicopter capable of night and all weather dipping sonar operations by virtue of its Louis Newmark autopilot and cable hover system. A total of 129 HAS1 models were delivered, some of which were used in the commando role for service in the Far East during the confrontation against Indonesia in the early 1960s. Operating from forward air bases such as NAANGA GAT, the Wessex of 845 and 848 Squadrons gave extensive support to the RM and Army in the jungles of Borneo. 3 Helicopters were built to the improved HAS3 standard and 43 converted from HAS1s (nearly all from commando units as these were replaced by the HU5). This model featured radar and improved sonar and flight control systems. In an attempt to cope with the increased weight these caused, the engine was uprated but the HAS3 proved a failure in front line service and the more capable Sea King airframe was ordered since it offered considerably more endurance with the same avionics. The HU5 entered service in 1964 as a specialist troop transport and load carrying version capable of carrying underslung loads of roughly 1½ tons in average conditions. 100 were delivered and these differed from the HAS versions in having 2 x Rolls Royce coupled Gnome 110/111 shaft turbine engines. In 1982, the HAS1 passed into history but the HAS3, which was due to be retired in early 1982, was retained for use in the Falklands Campaign. The HU5 was widely used in the Falklands Crisis with 847 and 848 Squadrons being reformed, with aircraft brought out of storage, to reinforce 845 Squadron. 848 lost its aircraft when the Atlantic Conveyor was sunk and 847 remained as part of the initial Falkland Island Garrison. 847 squadron was absorbed back into 845 squadron in 1983. 845 was re-equipped with Sea King HC4's in 1986 leaving a small number of Wessex in 771 and 772 squadrons for use in the training, SAR and second line utility roles. No immediate replacement is foreseen for these few remaining airframes

17 May 1957	Prototype Wessex (XL722) flew (actually a Sikorsky S58 experimentally fitted with a Napier Gazelle free power turbine)
20 June 1958	The first Westland built Wessex (XL727) flew
June 1960	700H Trials Flight formed at RNAS CULDROSE
4 July 1961	815, the first Wessex Squadron, commissioned at RNAS CULDROSE
31 May 1963	Prototype HU5 (XS241) first flew
5 December 1963	700V Trials Flight formed at RNAS CULDROSE
1966	845 Squadron re-equipped with HU5s
1967	814 Squadron re-equipped with HAS3s
1970	814 Squadron disbanded
1971	819, the last front line HAS3 Squadron, re-equipped with Sea Kings
9 August 1979	771, last HAS1 Squadron, re-equipped with HU5s

The last helicopter to take off from HMS ARK ROYAL (XS881) a HAS1 is preserved in the FAA Museum together with a HAS3 (XP142) which served in HMS ANTRIM in the South Atlantic Campaign

WESSEX HAS3 of 814 squadron landing on HMS HERMES. Note the team ready to connect a fuel hose to it.

E
ROYAL NAVY
A
DANGER

WESSEX helicopters have saved many lives in the SAR role over the last 21 years. This HAS 1 was formerly ship's flight of HMS ARK ROYAL; it was the last aircraft ever to leave her deck and can now be seen in the FAA Museum.

◁ WESSEX HU5 of 848 Squadron overflies HMS ALBION with an underslung 105 mm field gun.

WESTLAND WASP

Variants HAS1
Role Anti-submarine strike, light communication or SAR helicopter
Engine 1 x 710 shp Rolls Royce Nimbus 103 shaft turbine
Rotor Diameter 32′3″ **Length** 40′4″ **Max Weight** 5,500 lbs.
Max Speed 100 knots **Crew** Pilot, Aircrewman and 3 seats
Armament 2 x Mk44 or 46 homing torpedoes, 2 Mk11 depth charges, 4 SS11 or 2 x AS12 wire guided missiles all carried externally
Squadron Servica 829, 845, 848, 700, 703 and 706 Squadrons. BRNC DARTMOUTH Flight
Notes Designed by Saunders Roe as the P531, Wasps were built at the Fairey Aircraft Works at Hayes, Middlesex after that Company's absorption into Westland Helicopters. The Wasp was the first helicopter in the world designed specifically to operate from the decks of frigates and the RN received a total of 98 from 1963 onwards. From 1977 onwards it is gradually being replaced on warship decks by the Westland Lynx but when this replacement is complete it will still be retained for service in survey ships. Recommissioning of old frigates from the disposal list for the Falklands Crisis meant Wasp Flights being recommissioned as well and will delay the final demise of the front line Wasp force. The type has been exported to Holland, South Africa, Brazil, Indonesia and New Zealand. 829 is the Headquarters Squadron for the Wasp at RNAS PORTLAND detaching flights to ships at sea. For a time, some commando squadrons operated a single Wasp for reconnaissance duties but these were withdrawn in 1972

July 1958	Saunders Roe P531 started flight trials
28 October 1958	First Wasp (XS463) flew
July 1963	700W Trials Flight formed at RNAS CULDROSE
11 November 1963	First Ship's Flight commissioned for HMS LEANDER
5 March 1964	829 Squadron commissioned at RNAS CULDROSE
November 1964	829 Squadron moved to RNAS PORTLAND
27 February 1972	703 Training Squadron commissioned at RNAS PORTLAND
19 December 1980	703 Squadron disbanded transferring training task back to 829 Squadron

The Saunders Roe P531 prototype (XN332) is on display at the FAA Museum

WASP HAS 1 of 829 Squadron "AURORA" flight lands on it's parent frigate.

422
ROYAL NAVY
422
ROYAL NAVY
XT 420

WESTLAND SEA KING

Variants HAS1, HAS2, AEW2, HC4, HAS5
Role Anti-submarine search and strike, commando assault and SAR helicopter
Details are for HAS 5
Engine 2 x 1600 shp Rolls Royce Gnome H 1400-1
Rotor Diameter 62′0″ **Length** 54′9″ **Max Weight** 21,400 lbs.
Max Speed 120 knots **Crew** 2 Pilots, Observer and Aircrewman. Various passenger seats according to role. HC4 can carry up to 28 troops
Armament 4 fuselage hardpoints each capable of carrying Stingray, Mk46 or Mk44 torpedoes or Mk11 depth charges. A general purpose machine gun can be mounted in the cargo door. Various flares, markers, grenades and sonobuoys can be carried internally and hand launched.
Squadron Service 810, 814, 819, 820, 824, 825, 826, 845, 846, 849, HQ, 849A, 849B, 700S, 706 and 737 squadrons
Notes With the magnificent Sea King the helicopter came of age in the RN. Outstanding in its primary anti-submarine role it has excellent capabilities for long range search and rescue, troop transport and external load lifting. The basic airframe is a licence built version of the Sikorsky SH3D but the engines and mission equipment are all British. The anti-submarine equipment has been constantly updated to keep abreast of the threat and the HAS5 currently in production has active dipping sonar, passive sonobuoy monitoring equipment and the highly sophisticated "Sea Searcher" radar. Sea Kings can operate in the most atrocious weather and have constantly been in the news for dramatic rescues in the South West Approaches. It is fair to say that the Sea King played a key role in the Falklands Operation, protecting the Task Force at sea, ferrying men, stores and ammunition between ships before the San Carlos landing and supporting them ashore afterwards. A replacement, at present with the project number EH101 is planned to be produced jointly by Westland Helicopters and Augusta of Italy. If it goes ahead it is most unlikely to be available for squadron service before the early 1990s. The Sea King will continue therefore to form the backbone of the medium helicopter force for the foreseeable future and it is indeed still in production with many more orders expected to replace the losses from the Falklands Campaign. To date the RN has received 109 and the type has been a considerable export success, equipping the Navies of Australia, Belgium, Norway, Germany, Pakistan, India, and Egypt. An improved anti-submarine version, the HAS6 is in development for service in the 1990's. At the height of the Falklands War, two Sea Kings were modified for the airborne early warning role with the installation of the Thorn/EMI Searchwater radar system. The conversion took only 11 weeks and was so conspicuously successful that a further 8 airframes have been modified to restore the vital AEW capability to the fleet. A flight of 3 Seaking AEW helicopters now forms part of each front line air group

7 May 1969	First production HAS1 (XV642)flew
August 1969	700S IFTU commissioned at RNAS CULDROSE
February 1970	824, the first front line Squadron, commissioned at RNAS CULDROSE for service in HMS ARK ROYAL
June 1976	First HAS2 delivered
July 1982	First HAS2 modified for AEW role
November 1984	849 HQ reformed with Sea Kings at RNAS CULDROSE
August 1985	849 A flight embarked in HMS ILLUSTRIOUS

SEAKING AEW Mk2 of 849 A Flight.

SEAKING HC4 of 845 Squadron embarks Marines onboard HMS ARK ROYAL.

WESTLAND LYNX

Variants HAS2 HAS3
Role Anti-submarine strike, surface search and strike, search and rescue helicopter
Engine 2 x 900 shp Rolls Royce Gem BS 360-07-26
Rotor Diameter 42′0″ **Length** 39′1¼″ **Max Weight** 9,500 lbs.
Max Speed 150 knots **Crew** Pilot, Observer and up to 10 Passengers
Armament External pylons can carry up to 2 x Mk44, Mk46 or Stingray torpedoes, up to 4 x Sea Skua air to surface guided missiles, up to 2 x Mk11 depth charges or combinations of flares and markers
Squadron Service 815, 829, 700L and 702 Squadrons
Notes Second of the types produced by the Anglo French Helicopter agreement of 1967 to see service with the RN, the Lynx will ultimately replace the Wasp in small ships' flights. It is very much more capable than the Wasp in the surface warfare role using its Sea Spray radar to illuminate targets for the Sea Skua semi-active homing missiles. A number of hits were obtained with this system against a variety of targets in the Falklands action. Somewhat surprisingly the Lynx carries no submarine detection equipment although this may be remedied if trials with Magnetic Anomoly Detector equipment are successful. 702 is the Training Squadron for all Lynx aircrew and 815 and 829 are the headquarters squadrons, specialising in anti-surface vessel and anti-submarine warfare respectively. All are now based at RNAS PORTLAND after some years at RNAS YEOVILTON. Lynx have been exported to the Navies of Holland, France, West Germany, Norway, Denmark, Argentina and Nigeria with the possibility of more sales to follow. The IFTU, 700L Squadron was unusual in having both British and Dutch crews in order to expedite entry into service with both Navies. The AH1 variant is in front line service with the Army Air Corps

20 May 1972	First naval prototype (XX469) flew
September 1976	700L IFTU formed at RNAS YEOVILTON
December 1977	700L disbanded and recommissioned as 702 Squadron at RNAS YEOVILTON
29 January 1981	815 Squadron commissioned at RNAS YEOVILTON
July 1982	702 and 815 Squadrons moved to RNAS PORTLAND
July 1982	First HAS3 with uprated engines delivered to 815 Squadron

LYNX HAS2 of HMS AVENGER flight armed with a torpedo.

Purdy
341
ROYAL NAVY

SECOND LINE AIRCRAFT

AIRSPEED OXFORD

Variants T1
Role Trainer and utility
Engine 2 x 370 hp Armstrong Siddeley Cheetah X
Span 53′4″ **Length** 34′6″ **Max Weight** 8,000 lbs.
Max Speed 165 knots **Crew** 2 Pilots and up to 4 Passengers
Armament Nil
Squadron Service 762, 778, 782 and 792 Squadrons. Various Station Flights
Notes The Oxford saw fairly widespread service with the RN during World War II in a variety of second line roles. All were from RAF stocks with none built for the RN. Retained in large numbers after 1945, the type was not retired until 1954

OXFORD in wartime finish.

ANSON being used as a radar trainer for observers.

SECOND LINE AIRCRAFT

AVRO ANSON

Variants T1
Role Pilot instrument and observer trainer, communications
Engine 2 x 350 hp Armstrong Siddeley Cheetah IX
Span 56′6″ **Length** 42′3″ **Max Weight** 8,000 lbs.
Max Speed 165 knots **Crew** 1 or 2 Pilots plus 6 Passengers
Armament Nil
Squadron Service 750, 762, 771 and 783 Squadrons. Various Station Flights
Notes A small number of Ansons were taken on charge from RAF stocks after 1945. The last Anson was retired from RNAS LOSSIEMOUTH Station Flight in 1955

BEECH EXPEDITOR

Variants C2
Role Light communications and utility
Engine 2 x 450 hp Pratt and Whitney Wasp Junior
Span 47′8″ **Length** 34′3″ **Max Weight** 7,850 lbs.
Max Speed 200 knots **Crew** Pilot and 8 Passengers
Armament Nil
Squadron Service 728 Squadron. Various Station Flights
Notes 80 of these US aircraft were supplied to the RN during World War II under Lend/Lease arrangements. Most were returned or destroyed in 1945 but a few survived for use as "hacks" in the post war era. All were scrapped by 1954

EXPEDITOR of 728 Squadron from RNAS Hal Far, Malta.

SEA BALLIOLS from 727 Squadron, the Junior Officer's Air Course.

BOULTON PAUL SEA BALLIOL

Variants T21
Role Trainer and air experience
Engine 1 x 1,280 hp Rolls Royce Merlin 35
Span 39′4″ **Length** 35′1½″ **Max Weight** 8,410 lbs.
Max Speed 250 knots **Crew** 2 Pilots
Armament Nil
Squadron Service 702, 727, 750, 781, 1834, 1840, 1841 and 1843 Squadrons. Maintenance Test Pilot School, RNAS ABBOTSINCH
Notes A navalised version of the RAF Balliol, the Sea Balliol was fully equipped for deck landing and take-off and had a lively performance. 30 examples were delivered between October 1952 and December 1954. It was used for a variety of second line tasks including the Junior Officers' Air Course (JOAC) which set out to give young officers first hand experience of carrier aviation. Few of these aircraft survived the cutbacks that followed the 1957 Defence White Paper. One (WL732) can be seen at Cosford Aerospace Museum

BRITISH AEROSPACE JETSTREAM

Variants T2
Role Observer trainer
Engine 2 x 940 shp Astazou 16D turboprops
Span 52′0″ **Length** 48′1½″ **Max Weight** 13,230 lbs.
Max Speed 270 knots **Crew** 1 or 2 Pilots, 2 Student Observers and 3 other seats
Armament Nil
Squadron Service 750 Squadron
Notes 16 of these aircraft were converted from surplus RAF Jetstream T1 multi-engined pilot training aircraft, and issued to 750 Squadron in 1979 to replace the aged Sea Prince. A further four T3 aircraft were built for the Royal Navy for delivery in 1986. They differ in having a larger, 360 degree scanning radar fitted under the fuselage. Observers are trained initially on the Jetstream before going on to operational training in the specialist squadrons for each aircraft type. It was hoped to buy a limited number of Jetstream transports to replace the Sea Herons and Sea Devons in 781 Squadron but this failed to get political approval

JETSTREAM T2 of 750 Squadron.

TIGER MOTH over RNAS Lossiemouth.

SECOND LINE AIRCRAFT

DE HAVILLAND TIGER MOTH

Variants T1
Role Light trainer and pilot grader. Glider tug
Engine 1 x 130 hp de Havilland Gipsy Major
Span 29′4″ **Length** 23′11″ **Max Weight** 1,770 lbs.
Max Speed 95 knots **Crew** 2 Pilots
Armament Nil
Squadron Service 767 and 781 Squadrons. BRNC DARTMOUTH Air Experience Flight, Roborough. Various Station Flights
Notes Used by the FAA for a variety of training and "hack" roles between 1945 and the late 1960s. They were the workhorse of the Dartmouth Air Experience Flight until they were replaced by Chipmunks in 1965 and as such were the first aircraft flown by many generations of naval aviators. One example (XL717) is on display in the FAA Museum and a second (T8191) is airworthy with the RN Historic Flight at RNAS YEOVILTON

DE HAVILLAND DOMINIE

Variants C1
Role Communications
Engine 2 x 200 hp de Havilland Gipsy 6
Span 48′0″ **Length** 34′6″ **Max Weight** 5,500 lbs.
Max Speed 130 knots **Crew** Pilot, Aircrewman and 9 Passengers
Armament Nil
Squadron Service 778, 781, 782 and 783 Squadrons. Various Station Flights
Notes The RN acquired a total of 65 Dominies from 1940 onwards. During the war these were requisitioned civil aircraft but later aircraft were built for the FAA. The last examples were phased out in 1963

DOMINIE communications aircraft.

Naval CHIPMUNKS fitted for glider towing.

SECOND LINE AIRCRAFT

DE HAVILLAND CHIPMUNK

Variants T20
Role Light trainer and pilot grader. Glider tug
Engine 1 x 145 hp de Havilland Gipsy Major 8
Span 34′4″ **Length** 25′8″ **Max Weight** 2,000 lbs.
Max Speed 120 knots **Crew** 2 Pilots
Armament Nil
Squadron Service 781 Squadron. BRNC DARTMOUTH Air Experience Flight, Roborough. Various Station Flights
Notes 12 of these aircraft were bought from RAF stocks in 1965 to replace the Tiger Moth. They remain in service with the BRNC Flight as they represent a cheap and reliable aircraft in which to assess the suitability of new entry officers as aircrew. Some are used as weekend glider tugs at air stations. No replacement is in prospect

DE HAVILLAND SEA DEVON

Variants C20
Role Communications and fishery protection patrol
Engine 2 x 340 hp de Havilland Gipsy Queen 70
Span 57′0″ **Length** 39′0″ **Max Weight** 8,500 lbs.
Max Speed 180 knots **Crew** Pilot, Aircrewman and 8 Passengers
Armament Nil
Squadron Service 781 Squadron and Various Station Flights
Notes 13 of these splendid workhorses have been in service since 1955 with no sign of a replacement at present. They are used for fishery protection patrols as well as communication flights between air stations

SEA DEVON of RNAS Yeovilton's Heron Flight. Note the 'Cap Tally' on the tail.

SEA HERON on RNAS Yeovilton Station Flight Dispersal.

SECOND LINE AIRCRAFT

DE HAVILLAND SEA HERON

Variants C20
Role Communications
Engine 4 x 250 hp de Havilland Gipsy Queen 30
Span 71′6″ **Length** 48′6″ **Max Weight** 13,500 lbs.
Max Speed 160 knots **Crew** Pilot, Aircrewman and 14 Passengers
Armament Nil
Squadron Service 781 Squadron and Yeovilton Station Flight
Notes In service since 1961, 5 of these small airliners have given splendid value for money. All were bought second hand, 2 from Jersey Airlines, 2 from West African Airways and one was formerly in the Queen's Flight. They will continue to operate a communication service between naval air stations for the foreseeable future. The replacement of even these lowly machines is the subject of political debate and does not look very likely

ENGLISH ELECTRIC CANBERRA

Variants U10 T4 TT18 T22
Role Target tug and fleet requirements
Details are for TT18
Engine 2 x 6,500 lb. thrust Rolls Royce Avon
Span 63′11″ **Length** 65′6″ **Max Weight** 30,000 lbs.
Max Speed 475 knots **Crew** Pilot and Observer
Armament Nil
Squadron Service 728 and 776 Squadrons. Fleet Requirements and Aircraft Direction Training Unit (FRADU) at RNAS YEOVILTON
Notes These aircraft are all conversions of RAF Canberra B2 bombers and are operated for the RN on contract out of RNAS YEOVILTON by Airwork Services Limited with civilian aircrew and maintainers. Canberra U10s were used as targets for surface to air guided missile tests in the late 1950s operated by 728 Squadron out of RNAS HAL FAR in Malta. TT18s began to replace Meteors on more conventional target towing duties with 776 FRU at Hurn Airport, Bournemouth in 1970. In 1972 the unit moved to RNAS YEOVILTON and amalgamated with the civilian manned Hunters operating in support of the Air Direction School to form FRADU. Most Canberras operate towing Rushton targets for ships working up in the Channel areas. A small number were modified with the Buccaneer's Blue Parrot radar in a different nose cone to carry out realistic strike simulations on ships working up. The T4 is a dual controlled training version of the basic aircraft. All Canberras are showing distinct signs of age and their replacement by Dassault FALCONS has begun. These new aircraft are not owned by the Royal Navy but are operated under charter by Flight Refuelling Ltd. It is probable that the last Canberra will be retired in the near future

CANBERRA T4 of FRADU parked at RNAS Yeovilton.

METEOR TT20 in front of the tower at RNAS Yeovilton.

SECOND LINE AIRCRAFT

GLOSTER METEOR

Variants F3 T7 TT20
Role Experimental jet, pilot trainer, target tug and fleet requirements
Details are for T7
Engine 2 x 3,600 lb. thrust Rolls Royce Derwent 8
Span 37′2″ **Length** 43′6″ **Max Weight** 14,230 lbs.
Max Speed 510 knots **Crew** 2 Pilots (TT20 Pilot and Winch Operator)
Armament Nil
Squadron Service 703, 728, 759, 771, 776 and 778 Squadrons. Various Station Flights
Notes Two Meteor 3s were fitted with arrester hooks for deck landing experiments in HMS IMPLACABLE in 1948. They were the first twin jet aircraft ever to land on a carrier. 28 T7s were procured in the early 1950s, some new and some ex RAF. None were equipped for deck landing and they were operated mainly by 728 Squadron from RNAS HAL FAR in Malta and the civilian manned 776 Fleet Requirements Unit at Hurn Airport. A number of ex RAF NF11 night fighters were converted to TT20 standard by Armstrong Whitworth. These were equipped with a winch capable of towing a variety of targets at the end of 6,000 ft. of cable. TT20s were used by 728 and 776 Squadrons alongside T7s. TT20s were replaced in service by Canberras in the early 1970s. A T7 (WS103) and a TT20 (WM292) are preserved by the FAA Museum

HAWKER HUNTER

Variants T8 T8M GA11
Role Advanced pilot trainer, conversion trainer and weapon delivery trainer
Details are for T8
Engine 1 x 7,575 lb. thrust Rolls Royce Avon 122
Span 33′8″ **Length** 48′10½″ **Max Weight** 25,000 lbs.
Max Speed 620 knots **Crew** 2 Pilots (GA11 1 Pilot)
Armament 1 x Aden 30 mm cannon in early T8s. All variants have 4 underwing hardpoints each capable of carrying 1,000 lb. or practice bombs or 2″ rocket pods. T8M can carry Sidewinder air to air missiles on outboard pylons. All can carry 230 gallon drop tanks on inboard and 100 gallon drop tanks on outboard pylons
Squadron Service 738, 759 and 764 Squadrons. FRADU and various Station Flights
Notes In the late 1950s the RN bought 71 surplus Hunter F4 aircraft from the RAF at what now seems the bargain price of £30,000 each. These have given outstanding service to the FAA for more than 20 years as pilot training and fleet requirements aircraft. 10 RAF Hunter T7s were converted to T8 standard for the RN on the production line. 3 T8s have recently been converted to T8M standard with Sea Harrier type Blue Fox radar and head up display for pilot conversion training. Hunters will continue in service with FRADU and RN Standards Flight at RNAS YEOVILTON for the foreseeable future

3 March 1958	Prototype T8 (WW664) first flew
June 1962	First GA11 delivered
July 1975	Blue Herons display team formed. This was unique as civilian pilots were used flying service aircraft. This has now been disbanded

HUNTER T8 of 759 Squadron, based at RNAS BRAWDY.

BY
800

HILLER

Variants HTE2 HT2
Role Helicopter pilot trainer
Details are for HT2
Engine 1 x 305 hp Avco Lycoming VO540 B2D
Rotor Diameter 35′5″ **Length** 28′0″ **Max Weight** 2,750 lbs.
Max Speed 70 knots **Crew 2 Pilots and 1 Passenger**
Armament Nil
Squadron Service 845 and 705 Squadrons
Notes 20 HTE2 helicopters were provided by the USN under the Mutual Defence Aid Programme in 1953 and were used for ten years to convert pilots onto helicopters. They were replaced in 1963 by 21 HT2s purchased from the USA for the same role. These machines provided the first experience of rotary wing flight for the expanding numbers of specialist helicopter pilots that trained in the 1960s. Some HTE2s were used operationally in the Borneo confrontation by 845 Squadron in the light observation and communications role. Hillers were replaced by Gazelles in 1975. A Hiller HT2 (XB480) can be seen in the FAA Museum

HILLER 12E of 705 Squadron from RNAS Culdrose.

SEA PRINCES (T1) of 750 Squadron from RNAS CULDROSE.

SECOND LINE AIRCRAFT

HUNTING PERCIVAL SEA PRINCE

Variants C1 C2 T1
Role Communications, VIP transport and observer trainer
Engine 2 x 550 hp Alvis Leonides 125
Span 56′0″ **Length** 46′4″ **Max Weight** 11,850 lbs.
Max Speed 220 knots **Crew** Pilot plus 8 Passengers in communications versions (T1 Pilot, Observer and 3 Students)
Armament Nil
Squadron Service 750, 781 and 1841 Squadrons. Various Station Flights
Notes The RN ordered examples of the Sea Prince a good 3 years before the similar Pembroke was ordered by the RAF. 4 C1 models were followed by 42 T1s. The latter equipped 750 Observer Training Squadron for more than a quarter of a century during which period it was based at RN Air Stations CULDROSE, HAL FAR (Malta), LOSSIEMOUTH and finally CULDROSE again. Production ended with 3 C2 models, a communications variant of the T1

24 March 1950 First Sea Prince (WF136) flew
28 June 1951 First T1 (WF118) flew
3 September 1953 Last Sea Prince (WJ350) delivered
April 1979 Sea Princes replaced by Jetstreams in 750 Squadron

Two C1s (WF137 and WM756) and a C2 (WJ350) are in storage at the FAA Museum. A number of T1s found their way into Aircraft Preservation Groups and Museums after 1979

MARTIN BALTIMORE

Variants Mk4
Role Fleet requirements and utility
Engine 2 x 1600 hp Wright Cyclone R-2600-29
Span 61′4″ **Length** 48′6″ **Max Weight** 27,850 lbs.
Max Speed 280 knots **Crew** Pilot and up to 3 Passengers
Armament Nil
Squadron Service 728 Squadron
Notes Built in the US for service with the RAF. A small number of ex-RAF machines were passed on to the RN as replacements for the wartime Martin Maryland utility aircraft. All were withdrawn from service by 1947 after use mainly in the Mediterranean

This rare photograph shows a Naval BALTIMORE of 728 Squadron.

A MARTINET TT1 about to drop a target (with evident bullet holes in it) onto the deck of HMS VENGEANCE.

SECOND LINE AIRCRAFT

MILES MARTINET

Variants TT1
Role Target tug
Engine 1 x 870 hp Bristol Mercury XX
Span 39′0″ **Length** 30′11″ **Max Weight** 6,600 lbs.
Max Speed 200 knots **Crew** Pilot and Winch Operator
Armament Nil
Squadron Service 728, 736 and 771 Squadrons
Notes Used extensively by the RN during World War II, the Martinet was only gradually replaced after 1945 by more modern types such as the Sturgeon. This was due to its simplicity and economy of operation. The last examples were withdrawn in 1953

NORTH AMERICAN HARVARD

Variants T2A T2B T3
Role Pilot trainer
Engine 1 x 550 hp Pratt and Whitney Wasp
Span 42′0″ **Length** 29′0″ **Max Weight** 5,250 lbs.
Max Speed 180 knots **Crew** 2 Pilots
Armament Nil
Squadron Service 727, 771, 780, 781, 1830, 1831, 1832, 1833 and 1840 Squadrons. Various Station Flights
Notes Vast numbers of these basic trainers were supplied to the Commonwealth under Lend/Lease during World War II. Many found their way to the RN and some were retained post war for utility training duties. 2 examples have recently been recovered from the Portuguese Air Force and one (EX976) is on display at the FAA Museum. The other is in storage

HARVARD from RNAS Bramcote.

STURGEON TT2 being given the "cut" by the LSO seconds before landing on.

SECOND LINE AIRCRAFT

SHORT STURGEON

Variants BR1 (prototype only) TT2 TT3
Role Fleet target tug
Engine 2 x 1,660 hp Rolls Royce Merlin 140S
Span 59′9″ **Length** 48′10½″ **Max Weight** 22,350 lbs.
Max Speed 325 knots **Crew** Pilot and Observer/Aircrewman
Armament Nil
Squadron Service 728 and 771 Squadrons
Notes The Sturgeon was originally designed as a bomber reconnaissance aircraft for use in the new fleet carriers being built for the RN at the end of the War. The majority of these were cancelled and with them the BR1 model although the prototype flew in 1946. This showed promise and 2 prototypes and 23 production TT2s were built as target tugs for use by the Mediterranean Fleet. This version was fully capable of carrier operations and featured a grotesque long nose which housed cameras to film firings. Used mainly by 728 Squadron from RNAS HAL FAR in Malta, Sturgeons were used for general fleet requirement tasks as well as towing targets for surface to air and air to air firings. 19 aircraft were converted to TT3 standard with deck landing and photographic equipment deleted

1946	Prototype BR1 (RK787) flew
1 September 1949	Prototype TT2 (VR363) flew
8 June 1950	First production aircraft (TS475) delivered
May 1957	Last TT3 conversion delivered

Late 1950s superseded by Meteor TT20s

SIKORSKY HOVERFLY

Variants HR1 HR2
Role Utility, training and communications helicopter
Details are for HR2
Engine 1 x 245 hp Franklin piston
Rotor Diameter 38′0″ **Length** 47′11″ **Max Weight** 2,600 lbs.
Max Speed 80 knots **Crew** Pilot and 2 Passengers
Armament Nil
Squadron Service 705 and 771 Squadrons. Various Station and SAR Flights
Notes 67 were supplied to the RN under wartime Lend/Lease arrangements. These were the first rotary wing aircraft to service with the FAA and some continued in use post war until replaced by Dragonflies in 1950. Used mainly for experiments and developing the art of heliborne search and rescue

HOVERFLY being launched at Portland Naval Base.

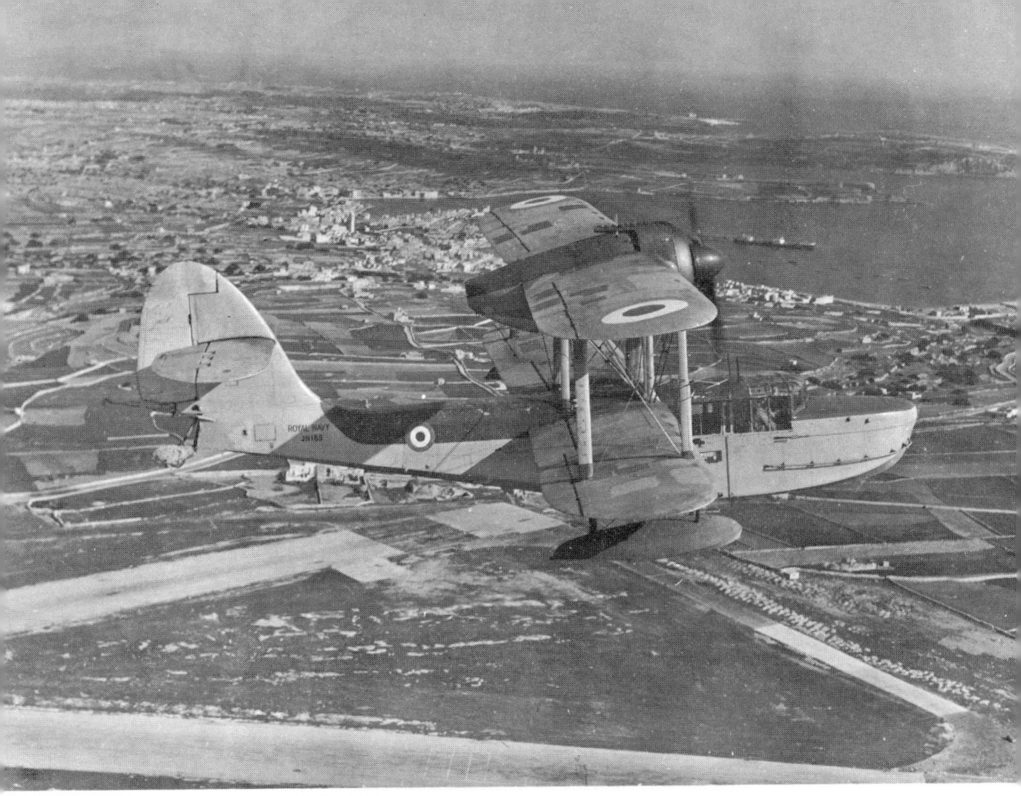

SEA OTTER over RNAS Hal Far.

SECOND LINE AIRCRAFT

SUPERMARINE SEA OTTER

Variants ASR2
Role Air-Sea Rescue and communications amphibian
Engine 1 x 855 hp Bristol Mercury XXX radial
Span 46′0″ **Length** 39′5″ **Max Weight** 10,250 lbs.
Max Speed 240 knots **Crew** Pilot, Observer and 2 Passengers
Armament Vickers K machine guns could be mounted, 1 amidships and 1 in bows
Squadron Service 772 and 781 Squadrons. Various Station Flights
Notes The last Supermarine amphibian, the Sea Otter began to replace the Walrus in search and rescue units in 1944. Small flights operated the aircraft both from carriers and air stations until helicopters took over the role in the early 1950s

August 1938	First prototype (K8854) flew
July 1943	Production run undertaken by Saunders Roe
July 1946	Last of 290 aircraft delivered

WESTLAND DRAGONFLY

Variants HR1 HR3 HR5
Role Search and rescue helicopter
Engine 1 x 550 hp Alvis Leonides 50
Rotor Diameter 49′0″ **Length** 57′6½″ **Max Weight** 5,870 lbs.
Max Speed 90 knots **Crew** Pilot and Aircrewman
Armament Nil
Squadron Service 705 Squadron, BRNC DARTMOUTH Flight and Various Carrier and Air Station SAR Flights
Notes The value of the helicopter as a carrier borne planeguard was rapidly appreciated by the RN during the Korean War and a small number of USN Sikorsky S51s were detached to British carriers off the west coast of Korea for SAR duties. A total of 72 S51s, known as Dragonflies, were built under licence by Westlands for the FAA. These served in every carrier in commission in the 1950s and also replaced Sea Otters in SAR Flights at air stations. They were in turn replaced by Whirlwinds in the late 1950s
September 1953 Last Dragonfly (WN500) was delivered
A Dragonfly HR5 (WN493) is preserved at the FAA Museum. Attempts to sell others as executive transports came to nothing and most have been scrapped

DRAGONFLY of Station Flight RNAS Lossiemouth.

GAZELLE of 705 Squadron display team 'The Sharks' from RNAS Culdrose.

SECOND LINE AIRCRAFT

WESTLAND GAZELLE

Variants HT2
Role Basic pilot training helicopter
Engine 1 x 592 shp Turbomeca Astazou
Rotor Diameter 34′5½″ **Length** 39′3¼″ **Max Weight** 3,970 lbs.
Max Speed 140 knots **Crew** 2 Pilots
Armament Nil
Squadron Service 705 Squadron
Notes One of the 3 helicopter types that resulted from the Anglo-French collaborative helicopter production agreement of 1967, the Gazelle is used in various roles by all the British Services. It is unusual in that the Intensive Flying Trials were carried out jointly by Army and RN personnel at the Army Air Corps Centre, Middle Wallop. The Gazelle replaced the Whirlwind 7 and Hiller as the basic helicopter trainer in 705 Squadron at RNAS CULDROSE. The first arrived in December 1974 and re-equipment was complete by March 1975. 30 Gazelles were delivered to the RN and they will continue to provide flying training up to "Wings" standard for the foreseeable future. 705 Squadron maintains a display team in the summer months known as "The Sharks" who are extremely well known at air displays throughout the country. The Royal Marines of 3 Commando Brigade Air Squadron fly the Army AH1 variant

CANCELLED PROJECTS

BRISTOL TYPE 191

Role Large anti-submarine helicopter
Engine 2 x Napier Gazelle free power turbines
Rotor Diameter 48′7″ **Length** 87′0″ **Max Weight** never finalised
Max Speed 120 knots **Crew** 2 Pilots, Observer and Aircrewman
Armament provision intended for 2 x Mk 30 torpedoes or depth charges
Notes Three versions of this tandem rotor helicopter were planned in the mid 1950s, the 191 fitted with dipping sonar for the RN, the 192 as a transport for the RAF and the 193, a slightly modified 191, for the Royal Canadian Navy. 68 Type 191s were ordered by the Admiralty in April 1956 but these were subsequently withdrawn as another victim of the 1957 Defence White Paper. The RCN order was also cancelled but the 192 eventually saw production and service with the RAF as the Belvedere. Whatever its merits might have been, the 191 would have been enormous and much more difficult to blend in with fixed wing operations on a carrier than the Wessex that subsequently took its place

BRISTOL type 173 prototype broadly similar to the Type 191 carrying out deck trials on HMS EAGLE.

The first prototype SPEARFISH.

CANCELLED PROJECTS

FAIREY SPEARFISH

Role Torpedo bomber and reconnaissance
Engine 1 x 2320 hp Bristol Centaurus 58, 59 or 60
Span 60′3″ **Length** 44′7″ **Max Weight** 22,083 lbs.
Max Speed 250 knots **Crew** Pilot and Observer
Armament Planned to have a single torpedo or up to 4 x 1,000 lb. or 500 lb. bombs or depth charges internally. 1 x 0.5″ Browning machine gun in a remotely controlled turret aft of the cockpit
Notes Massive by any standard, the Spearfish was intended as a replacement for the Barracuda. The production contract to Specification 05/43 was cancelled in 1946 but 3 examples flew and were used as "hacks" for a variety of tasks by the Carrier Trials Unit at RNAS FORD until the early 1950s

HAWKER P1052/P1081

Role Fighter
Engine 1 x 6250 lb. thrust Rolls Royce Tay
Span 36′6″ **Length** 44′0″ **Max Weight** 16,000 lbs.
Max Speed 560 knots **Crew** Pilot
Armament 4 x 20 mm cannon in nose. External provision planned for rockets and bombs
Notes Basically these two types were swept wing versions of the classic Sea Hawk. The P1052 retained the original Sea Hawk tail and as a result suffered from instability and a lower top speed. The P1081 had all swept flying surfaces and proved to have excellent handling qualities. The P1052 flew in December 1948 just two years after the RN ordered the straight wing P1040 Sea Hawk into production. A few senior officers with vision tried to get the more advanced aircraft ordered into production but more conservative views held sway with the Board of Admiralty and, despite continuing interest, these two types were never ordered into production and the RN had to wait until 1958 to get a swept wing fighter into service. The P1081 could have been in squadron service in 1952. It even carried out highly successful carrier trials on HMS EAGLE in May 1952 with VX272 but by then it was too late and the Sea Hawk was in full production. In retrospect it is clear that the RN missed a chance to purchase a fighter the equal of any in service instead of the pleasant but by international standards pedestrian Sea Hawk. The export market for carrier borne fighters passed irrevocably to the USA after the RN's failure to buy modern equipment in the early 1950s

P1052. Note the close resemblance to the SEAHAWK.

HAWKER SIDDELEY P1154RN

Role Vertical/Short take off and landing all weather figher
Engine 1 x 35,600 lb. Bristol Siddeley BS100/8 vectored thrust turbofan with Plenum Chamber Burning
Span 30′0″ **Length** 59′0″ **Max Weight** 40,000 lbs.
Max Speed MACH 2 **Crew** Pilot and Observer
Armament 4 x Red Top infra-red seeking air to air guided missiles on underwing pylons. Provision was planned for these pylons to carry drop tanks or 1,000 lb. bombs or AS30 air to ground missiles in the strike role
Notes The P1154 was conceived as a ground attack fighter to meet a NATO Military requirement. In 1963 the Minister of Defence insisted that the design should form a basis for the RAF Hunter replacement and the RN Sea Vixen replacement. Since the RAF required a single seat, single engined low flying ground attack aircraft and the RN wanted a two seat, two engined high flying interceptor with an enormous radar and missile control system; the two roles were clearly incompatible and the idea was doomed from the start. This resulted in the RN ordering the USN Phantom in 1964 instead, leaving the P1154 as a purely RAF project which was eventually cancelled in 1965. With the recent success of the Sea Harrier in the Falklands fighting, one can only speculate as to the success of the P1154RN which we could have had in service from the early 1970s had the RN been allowed to develop it to its own requirements

---

CANCELLED PROJECTS

HAWKER SIDDELEY P139B

Roles Airborne early warning/carrier on board delivery/air to air refuelling tanker
Engine High bypass turbofans (type never finalised)
Span 50′0″ **Length** 45′0″ **Max Weight** 40,000 lbs. approx.
Max Speed 400 knots **Crew** 2 pilots and 2 Observers
Armament Nil planned
Notes Intended to serve in carriers of the CVA01 class, the P139B was designed by Hawker Siddeley Brough (formerly Blackburn Aircraft) in 1965. It was not unlike the USN Viking but with a more dumpy fuselage to accommodate the scanners for the new frequency modulated interrupted continuous wave (FMICW) Radar. Without the radar, the carrier on board delivery (COD) version would have had the nose faired in and a cone shaped side opening freight door aft giving access to a vast space for the carriage of stores, passengers and of course mail. This same utility version could have been fitted with extra fuel tanks giving the aircraft a first rate capability as an air to air refuelling tanker. When the CVA01 was axed in the 1966 Defence Review, the P139 was axed along with it though fortunately work on the FMICW radar continued at a low key and it forms the basis of the system to be fitted to the Nimrod AEW3 (the fore and aft scanners of which give scale to the dumpiness of the P139 fuselage). The terrible void in Naval capabilities caused by this short sighted cancellation was only too obvious in the Falklands operations

SAUNDERS ROE P177

Role Supersonic interceptor fighter
Engine 1 x de Havilland Gyron Junior DGJ10-1 turbojet with reheat plus 1 x de Havilland D SPE 5 rocket motor
Span 30′6″ **Length** 50′6″ **Max Weight** 28,174 lbs.
Max Speed Mach 2.5 **Crew** Pilot
Armament 2 x wing tip mounted Firestreak air to air guided missiles. Provision for strike weapons intended
Notes Another victim of the 1957 Defence Review the P177 was a futuristic design intended to achieve a phenominal performance with an internal rocket motor as well as a conventional reheated turbojet. It was intended for service with the RAF as well as the RN and West Germany was intensely interested in participating in the project. A design contract was signed in May 1955 and a contract for 27 aircraft including 5 initial prototypes was signed in September 1956. Development flying was planned to start in January 1958 but even though 5 prototypes were well advanced the project was cancelled in April 1957 and the uncompleted airframes mothballed (together with the SR53 development aircraft). One can only speculate as to what such an aircraft might have achieved. The dangers of handling the volatile rocket fuel on board a ship were never seriously addressed and would have led to very real problems had the P177 gone into production

SR 53 prototype showing how the P177 fighter would have appeared.

Rare photograph of the SEAMEW during carrier trials.

CANCELLED PROJECTS

SHORT SEAMEW

Variants AS1
Role Anti-Submarine search and strike
Engine 1 x Armstrong Siddeley Mamba
Span 55′0″ **Length** 41′0″ **Max Weight** 15,000 lbs.
Max Speed 200 knots **Crew** Pilot and Observer
Armament Internal weapon bay was designed to carry homing torpedoes, depth charges, sonobuoys etc.
Notes The Seamew was designed to specification M123 of 1951 for an unsophisticated anti submarine aircraft capable of operation from light fleet or escort carriers. The first prototype flew at RNAY SYDENHAM, Belfast in August 1953. Remarkably ugly and with a fixed undercarriage designed to be blown off in the event of a ditching becoming necessary it was seriously underpowered. One prototype XA213 completed carrier trials in HMS BULWARK in 1955. It was intended to buy a number of Seamews for RAF Coastal Command but this order ws cancelled in 1956 when deliveries of production aircraft to the RN started. The substantial RN order was also reduced and only 24 aircraft were delivered to the Aircraft Holding Unit at RNAS LOSSIEMOUTH for storage. The whole project was cancelled in the 1957 Defence White Paper and the airframes were scrapped together with the light carriers they were intended for

SUPERMARINE SEAFANG

Planned Variants F31 F32
Role Fighter
Engine 1 x 2,375 hp Rolls Royce Griffon 89
Span 35′0″ **Length** 34′1″ **Max Weight** 11,400 lbs.
Max Speed 420 knots **Crew** Pilot
Armament 4 x 20 mm Hispano Cannon in Wings
Notes The Seafang was a navalised version of the Spiteful, a Spitfire derivative intended for the RAF. 150 were ordered in May 1945 under the specification N5/45 but the order was cancelled after only 8 were delivered. These had unpleasant handling qualities and were used mainly for development flying concerned with the laminar flow wing which was to be used on the Attacker

SEAFANG shortly after delivery.

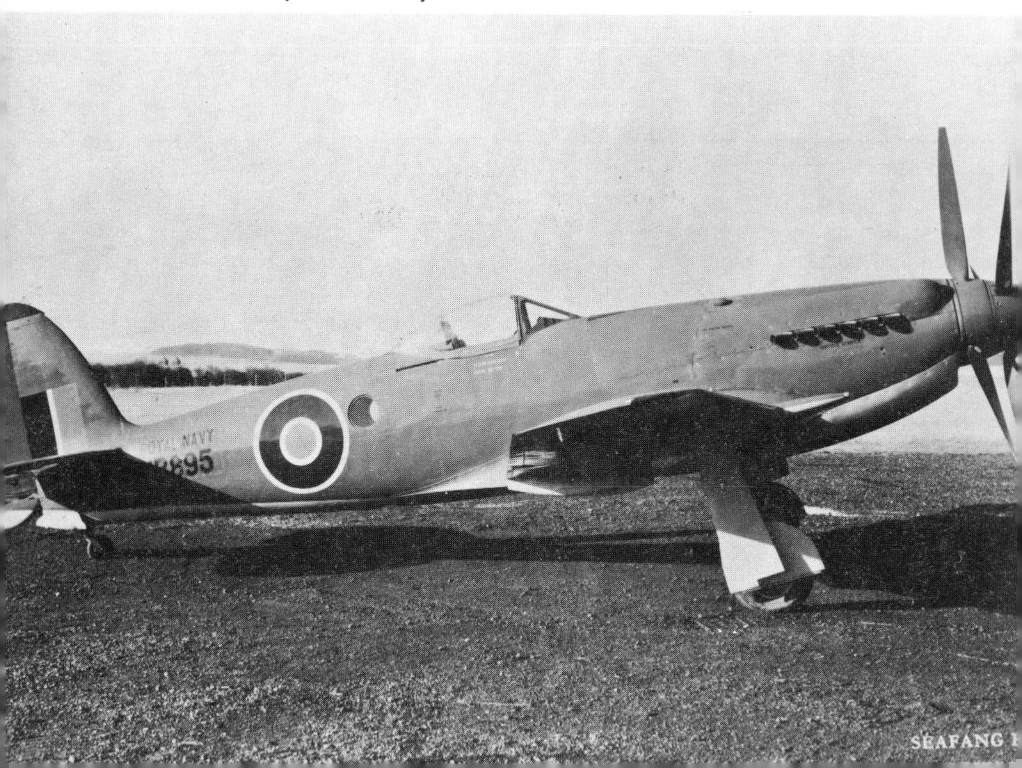

MILES MONITOR

Variants TT11
Role Target tug
Engine 2 x 1,750 hp Wright R-2600-31 Double Row Cyclone
Span 55′3″ **Length** 46′8″ **Max Weight** 21,000 lbs.
Max Speed 310 knots **Crew** Pilot and Aircrewman
Armament Nil
Notes The Monitor was originally designed for the RAF but cancelled. The TT11 was a modified version designed for the RN but with the end of the war in 1945 only 10 out of an order for 200 were delivered. These never saw service

MONITOR

PRESENT DAY AIRCRAFT CARRIERS, AIR STATIONS AND THEIR SQUADRONS (AS OF LATE 1987)

HMS ARK ROYAL

801 Squadron	Sea Harrier FRS 1
820 Squadron	Sea King HAS 5
849 A Flight	Sea King AEW 2

HMS ILLUSTRIOUS

800 Squadron	Sea Harrier FRS 1
814 Squadron	Sea King HAS 5
849A Flight	Sea King AEW 2

HMS INVINCIBLE

In extended refit, Devonport. No squadrons.

RNAS YEOVILTON (HMS HERON)

800 Squadron	Sea Harrier FRS 1	when disembarked
801 Squadron	Sea Harrier FRS 1	when disembarked
845 Squadron	Sea King HC 4	Commando Assault
846 Squadron	Sea King HC 4	Commando Assault
899 Squadron	Sea Harrier FRS 1	Headquarters and Training
707 Squadron	Sea King HC 4	Commando Training
Heron Flight	Sea Heron	Utility
	Chipmunk	
Naval flying	Hunter GA II	Standardisation and Instrument
Standards flight	Hunter T 8	training for fixed wing pilots
Fleet Requirements	Canberra	Fleet requirements and
and Aircraft	Falcon	fighter controller training
Direction Training	Hunter T 8	
Unit	Hunter GA 11	
RN	Swordfish	Preservation and Display of
Historic Flight	Sea Fury FB 11	old aircraft in flying condition
	Sea Fury T20	
	Firefly AS5	
	Tiger Moth	

RNAS CULDROSE (HMS SEA HAWK)

810 Squadron	Sea King HAS 5	Sea King operational training
814 Squadron	Sea King HAS 5	when disembarked
820 Squadron	Sea King HAS 5	when disembarked
824 Squadron	Sea King HAS 5	Trials (Due to move to Prestwick)
826 Squadron	Sea King HAS 5	provides flights for RFAs
849 HQ Flight	Sea King AEW 2	AEW Headquarters and training
849 A Flight	Sea King AEW 2	when disembarked
849 B Flight	Sea King AEW 2	when disembarked
705 Squadron	Gazelle HT 2	Pilot training to "wings" standard
706 Squadron	Sea King HAS 5	Sea King advanced training
750 Squadron	Jetstream T 2/T3	Observer training
771 Squadron	Wessex HU 5	SAR and Fleet Requirements

The School of Aircraft Handling uses a number of grounded airframes to practice aircraft movement.

RNAS PORTLAND (HMS OSPREY)

815 Squadron	Lynx HAS 2/3	Parenting for Lynx flights
829 Squadron	Wasp HAS 1 Lynx HAS 2/3	Parenting for Wasp and Lynx Flights
702 Squadron	Lynx HAS 2/3	Lynx operational training
772 Squadron	Wessex HU 5	SAR and Fleet Requirements

RNAS LEE-ON-SOLENT (HMS DAEDALUS)

LEE SAR Flight	Wessex HU 5	SAR

PRESTWICK AIRPORT (HMS GANNET)

819 Squadron	Sea King HAS 5	Anti-submarine and SAR

THE FOLLOWING AIRCRAFT ARE ON DISPLAY TO THE PUBLIC AT THE FLEET AIR ARM MUSEUM, RNAS YEOVILTON, SOMERSET

Albatross D Va (R)	G-BFXL
BAC 221	WG774
BAC Concorde 002	G-BSST
Beech T-34C Mentor	411
Bell UH-1H Iroquois	AE-422
Bensen Gyrocopter	G-AZAZ
Blackburn Buccaneer S.1	XN967
Blackburn NA.39	XK488
de Havilland D.H.82A Tiger Moth (Historic Flight)	T1891
de Havilland D.H.82A Tiger Moth	XL717
de Havilland D.H.100 Sea Vampire	LZ551/G
de Havilland D.H.110 Sea Vixen FAW.1	XJ481
de Havilland D.H.110 Sea Vixen FAW.2	XS590
de Havilland D.H.112 Sea Venom FAW.21	WW138
Douglas Skyraider AEW.1	WT121
Eclipse Eagle	G-BGWZ
Fairey Firefly TT.4	VH127
Fairey Flycatcher (R) (Winter only)	S1287
Fairey Fulmar 1	N1854
Fairey Gannet AEW.3	XL503
Fairey Gannet COD.4	XA466
Fairey Swordfish II	W5984
Fairey Swordfish II (Historic Flight)	LS326
FMA 1A 58A Pucara	A-522
Fokker Dr 1(R)	—
Gloster Sea Gladiator	N2276
Grumman Avenger AS.6	XB446
Grumman Hellcat II	KE209
Grumman Martlet 1	AL246
Handley Page H.P.115	XP841
Hawker Sea Fury FB.11	WJ231
Hawker Sea Hawk FGA.4	WV856
Hiller HT 1	XB480
Macchi MB.339	A110/116

North American AT-6D Harvard III	EX976
Saro P.531	XN332
Sopwith Baby	N2078
Sopwith Camel (R)	B6401
Sopwith Pup (R)	N6452
Supermarine Attacker F.1	WA472
Supermarine Scimitar F.1	XD317
Supermarine Seafire FR.17	SX137
Supermarine Walrus 1	L2301
Vought F4U-6 Corsair IV	KD431
Westland Dragonfly HR.5	WN493
Westland Sioux	XT176
Westland Wasp HAS.1	XT427
Westland Wesex HAS.1	XS881
Westland Wessex HAS.3	XP142
Westland Whirlwind HAR.1	XA864
Westland Whirlwind HAS.3	XJ402
Westland Wyvern TF-1	VR137
Yokosuka MXY-7 Ohka	—

The Museum also has the remains of Rutland of Jutland's Short 184, of Skua L2940, and the remains of Fairey Barracuda DP872, which are all on display. A World War One gallery is now open.

SEA HARRIER OF 809 Squadron at RNAS Yeovilton